AF324919

A WORLD OF SPORTS FOR GIRLS

"We won!"

Montgomery Newspapers

A WORLD OF SPORTS
FOR GIRLS

by
Gail Andersen Myers

The Westminster Press
Philadelphia

First edition

BOOK DESIGN BY ALICE DERR

Published by The Westminster Press®
Philadelphia, Pennsylvania

PRINTED IN THE UNITED STATES OF AMERICA
9 8 7 6 5 4 3 2 1

Library of Congress Cataloging in Publication Data

Myers, Gail Andersen, 1933–
 A world of sports for girls.

 Bibliography: p.
 Includes index.
 SUMMARY: Explores the opportunities now becoming available to female athletes in a wide variety of sports and sports-related careers.
 [1. Sports for women—Vocational guidance.
2. Vocational guidance] I. Title.
GV709.M93   796'.01'940973   81–10440
ISBN 0–664–32683–8   AACR2

Contents

Foreword

An exciting new world is opening to all girls who love sports. Today they can use their bodies and minds as they choose—for fun and exercise, for challenging competition or for stimulating careers.

To explore the opportunities now becoming available to female athletes, I talked to girls and women around the country who are actively involved in a wide variety of sports and sports-related careers.

They are not superstars—although they might be in the near future. They are people whose goals are reachable. All of them are courageous, dedicated, and hardworking.

I asked how they began, how they improved, what their hopes are. And I thank each and every one of them for so openly sharing their inspiring stories.

The best part about sports, of course, is not the watching, but the doing. Today's sportsgirl is eager to move on down the path of her choice. The good news is that she can keep moving along that path all through her life—today, tomorrow, and always.

1. Starting Out

As a Chinese philosopher once said, "A journey of a thousand miles must begin with a single step." For girls starting out on an athletic journey, the first step may be running.

Running is the simplest sport to start. A runner needs little equipment—just a pair of good shoes. She can run anywhere, on tracks, in parks, even on city streets. And she can run anytime, even in sleet, snow, or rain.

Today, millions of people across America are running. They come in all ages, sexes, shapes, and sizes. And their motives vary a great deal, too.

"To get rid of my flab" is the reason why many people take up running. But they strive for physical fitness, a strong heart and healthy lungs, as well as a flat stomach. Sometimes they endure monotony, pain, or injury, but they keep on running. And once they can log a mile or two without panting or aching, they proclaim to anyone who will listen: "Running makes me feel good!"

For some, that feeling is enough. They like to run their own distance at their own pace, with no one else keeping score. But for many, the thrill of running comes mainly while matching oneself against others—in a race.

Kim Gallagher, fourteen, just likes competition. She likes the feeling of coming in first in a race.

Today, at a Saturday track meet, Kim is leading the pack in

an 880-yard race. Although the temperature is over 90°F, she appears to run effortlessly at a steady pace.

A gray-haired man in the grandstand nudges his wife and points to a thin figure in a pale-blue tank top and shorts. "That's Kim Gallagher," he tells her. "She's a champion!"

The stands are full of people who hope their sons and daughters, brothers, sisters, and friends will be champions, too. They cheer for their favorites, shouting encouragement: "Come on, Cynthia!" "Pour it on, Lisa!" "Bring it in, Tanya!"

The meet is an important one, for the top three place winners in each event will go on to the Nationals in Maryland next month. Nevertheless, a circus atmosphere prevails. Two red-striped officials' tents in the middle of the field add to the mood.

Several different events are going on at the same time. Just inside the track, a ten-year-old long jumper sprints down a runway, touches down on a board, launches into the air, and lands in a pit of sand. At the far end of the field, pole vaulters try to conquer higher and higher bars, each time falling onto a bright-blue padded mat. In a nearby field, discus, shot put, and javelin throwers compete for coveted medals.

Excitement mounts as the runners in the 880 near the finish line. One girl wears a contorted look of pain on her face. Another gasps with exhaustion. But Kim Gallagher, maintaining the same controlled, concentrating expression she began the race with, strides gracefully across the finish line—first again.

Only later, as she steps onto the highest box of the three-tiered awards stand, does she break into a smile. Now she can relax and enjoy the cheers of the crowd, the feel of still another medal ribbon around her neck.

Kim has enjoyed this happy feeling many times before. In less than a year, she set an AAU (Amateur Athletic Union) national age-group record in the half mile (2 minutes, 11 seconds), won the National Junior Olympics half mile and two

"When I run, I feel good!" says Kim Gallagher
Montgomery Newspapers

UPPER DUB
5

mile races, won the Pennsylvania State Class AAA cross-country meet, and set a new record in the important Penn Relays by running a mile in 4:49.2.

According to her brother, Bart, Kim's trophy case at home contains one hundred twenty-five medals, seventy trophies, and "a few watches, plaques, and silver platters." Sixteen-year-old Bart is Kim's self-appointed press agent. He is also "coach away from coaches," timekeeper, manager, spokesman, chaperone, masseur, and number one fan all rolled into one.

"My brother really has a lot to do with my career," Kim declares after the race. "He's the one who got me interested in running and he gave up his own track career because of me. He was doing so much for me that he couldn't keep himself in mind. I feel very fortunate he's with me."

Kim's mother, who works in an avionics firm, and her father, a salesman, are also very supportive and enthusiastic. They attend most of the meets or send Bart to accompany Kim. However, her family and coaches try very hard not to pressure her or look too far in the future, lest she "burn out."

Although the sportswriters call her "Wonder Woman," Kim is only 5'3" tall and weighs 93 pounds at most. There is no flab on this runner and there probably never was.

"I've been running half my life," says the dark, wavy-haired ninth-grader. "I just always knew I had speed."

Kim put that speed to good use early—at the age of seven. She joined a track club in her hometown, Ambler, Pennsylvania. Two weeks later, she ran a 5:39 mile!

Since even many professional male athletes cannot break the six-minute mile barrier, Kim's coach, Larry Wilson, knew he had a rare talent on his hands. He set to work teaching Kim the basics of running—how to use her arms properly, how to hold her head, how to perfect her stride. And he found high-caliber competition for her.

AAU age-group competitions begin with the Bantams (ages 9 and under) and progress through Midgets (ages 10–11), Juniors (ages 12–13), Intermediates (ages 14–15), and Seniors (ages 16–17). The "open" competitions field 14- to 17-year-olds.

For many sports, competition on the local, national, and

international levels is sponsored by the AAU, "America's largest nonprofit volunteer service organization dedicated to the encouragement of amateur sports and physical fitness." Over twenty-five million Americans participate in AAU events each year through athletic clubs, high schools, colleges and universities, and civic, community, and fraternal organizations.

Generally in AAU programs, youngsters start out in age-group divisions. Success in one level of meets qualifies a participant to enter higher level competition. In individual sports, such as swimming or track, finishing in the top second or third position in a local meet qualifies a participant to enter a state meet, where she may qualify for a regional meet. Team sports, such as basketball, follow the same pattern.

Local, state, and regional meets lead to national Junior Olympics Championship competitions in each sport at various locations throughout the country.

Millions of girls and boys, aged eight through eighteen, participate every year in the AAU's Junior Olympics program in seventeen sports—basketball, bobsled, boxing, cross-country, decathlon/pentathlon, luge, swimming, volleyball, water polo, weight lifting, diving, gymnastics, judo, synchronized swimming, track and field, trampoline and tumbling, and wrestling. (Not all these sports are open to girls, however.)

As Kim Gallagher found out, the higher the level, the stiffer the competition. Even though Kim was called a track phenomenon in local meets, AAU competitions around the country were a different matter. She lost frequently, often became discouraged, and almost quit many times.

"I thought running would be fun, but I kept coming in last all the time," she remembers. "I used to stop running and just walk to the finish line because I got so frustrated. I wanted to quit the whole thing."

Just when she was most discouraged, she was entered in a race in Van Cortland Park in New York City. Coach Wilson sat her down and told her she had a good chance to win that race. He also did an extra job of salesmanship.

"He told me how big the trophy was," Kim recalls with a gleam in her dark-brown eyes. "It was bigger than me. When

Runners sometimes endure pain, but they keep on running

Montgomery Newspapers

I heard that, I really got anxious to win. And after I won that, I got interested in running again." The lure of that trophy gave her the boost she desperately needed.

She has had other boosts along the way, like the excitement of travel. She enjoyed a fun-packed visit to Disney World after competing in a meet nearby. Recently she had her first awe-inspiring glimpse of the Rocky Mountains when she participated in Sports Festival II in Colorado Springs as a member of the Eastern Track Team.

But Kim cautions other athletes not to expect every trip to

be exciting and glamorous. "Sometimes you just stay in a hotel, run a race, and go home," she says.

An unexpected bonus occasionally comes in the form of clothing and shoes from manufacturers who hope she will wear their emblems when she races. A lime green warm-up suit is her current favorite.

Like all athletes under AAU rules, Kim cannot accept money, but she can accept clothing or equipment gifts as well as sponsors' support for out-of-pocket expenses, such as transportation, food, and lodging.

According to Coach Wilson, expenses for the members of the track club can run $600–$800 apiece each season. Funds for high expenses, such as bus rental and insurance, are raised from private contributions. Parents' committees hold special sales of cakes, pencils, and even refrigerator deodorant and run refreshment concessions at meets to raise funds.

Cooperative sports clubs like the Ambler one are springing up in communities across the nation. They offer high-caliber coaching and competition for girls and boys of an earlier age than most school systems provide. Junior and senior high school coaches often do not have the time or expertise to give individual attention to promising young athletes. Some have never even played the sport they coach, but take on the job strictly for the additional pay.

Kim Gallagher was lucky to find a fine track club right in her hometown and a dedicated coach like Larry Wilson. Later, she was also lucky to find an experienced Upper Dublin High School coach named Jack Fuery, who "eats, drinks, and sleeps track."

While doing his best to keep the rest of the team motivated, Coach Fuery makes up original workouts for his superstar, Kim. He says of her, "Even though she's thin, she's powerful. She has a natural ability and she's a hard worker. I don't think she's ever missed a practice."

After her junior high school classes, Kim goes to the high school track to practice every day from 3 to 5 P.M. She participates on the cross-country team in the fall, runs indoor track in the winter and outdoor track in the spring.

Discus throwers compete for coveted medals at track and field meets

Montgomery Newspapers

From 5:30 to 7:30 P.M. all year around, she practices with the Olympic Club Monday through Thursday and also works out on Universal Gym equipment. Most weekends, she competes in meets.

Summers she also swims and plays a little tennis. "But I'm not very good at that yet," she admits while rubbing one of her tiny heart-shaped earrings. In between, she likes to "watch TV and eat."

Diet is no problem for this slim athlete. However, she has sometimes suffered from nervous stomach, nausea, and even vomiting at a meet. Now, to solve that problem, she always eats a hearty breakfast of pancakes before competing.

Although in running ability she is far ahead of most of her high school teammates and competitors, in age she is two to four years behind most of them. Does she get lonely?

"I like to run by myself," she answers thoughtfully. "When anyone comes out there with me, I try not to think about them. I just run my race."

The Olympics and college are Kim's private goals. Both goals are a long way off, because, hard as it is to believe, Kim is only fourteen years old. For the present, she just puts one foot in front of the other. Her strategy is simple: "I just run as fast as I can."

Kim started out in a local sports club. Other sports-minded people can find such a club by watching the local news of meets. While attending meets, they can gather information about the clubs to which participants belong.

Local Y's also offer clinics and group lessons in many sports on beginning as well as advanced levels. Millions of top-ranked athletes began learning their basic skills within these agencies.

Municipal recreation departments also provide clinics for beginners in many sports as well as competitions for advanced players. Telephone calls to these agencies will bring information on how to get started in their programs.

Besides teaching skills, group lessons and clinics provide practice partners. During lessons, a player can meet others on her ability level. She can make a date with a new friend to practice or play another time. Lessons are not enough—practice in between is essential to learning.

Of course, it is not always possible to get out and run or play or practice. Weather conditions or lack of practice facilities may intervene. Then one can read about sports.

Sports magazines offer tips for perfecting skills written by experts. Interviews with current sports stars provide inspiration. The monthly magazine *Runner's World,* for example, gives both inspiration and practical tips to serious competitive runners.

Organizations that govern each sport usually send newsletters or magazines to members. The National Jogging Association sends its members a newspaper that offers encouragement and information for those who run for fitness and fun.

The 796 section in every library contains books on athletics. Both the juvenile and adult sections have how-to-do-it books for every level of player, as well as biographies of outstanding players.

The vast majority of these books are written for, about, and by male athletes, however. Little attention has been paid to the special needs of female athletes, other than an occasional mention or a single chapter. Apparently girls are expected to learn to play "like the boys."

Today a change is slowly taking place on the library and bookstore shelves. Some books are appearing that direct their attention strictly to females. There are guides to women's track and field, golf, tennis, skiing, and other sports. At last the

Running the hurdles is seldom monotonous
Montgomery Newspapers

special needs of female athletes are beginning to be recognized in print.

Dr. Joan Ullyot, for example, has recently written a book called *Women's Running*. In it, Dr. Ullyot openly discusses topics special to women and girls, such as menstruation, pregnancy, and the need for a jogging bra.

Dr. Ullyot also recommends a doctor's checkup for beginning runners who have any health problem or are over forty. While clothing can be almost anything that is comfortable, she insists that proper shoes ($25–$30 road-running flats), rather than sneakers or loafers, are an absolute must.

To prevent injury, she also suggests a warm-up of gentle stretching exercises (toe-touching or hamstring stretch-and-hold) followed by a slow, easy jog for the first few minutes.

A confirmed long-distance runner herself, Dr. Ullyot stresses certain basic principles that apply to beginners, intermediates, and racers alike:

> Regularity in daily activity, even if only for twenty to thirty minutes

> Hard/easy pattern, because the body responds to a hard, stressful workout if it is given a chance to recuperate its gains the following day

> Distance over speed, because endurance is the necessary base for all running

The tracks, golf courses, and roads would soon be covered with happy, healthy, sweating runners if Dr. Ullyot had her way. She declares, "I'd like to see every man, woman, and child in America run his or her miles daily just as routinely as they brush their teeth.

"This would eliminate a lot of problems that result from sedentary life—boredom, tension, violence, that old bugaboo constipation, dependence on tranquilizers, alcohol, cigarettes, and other drugs. Utopia could be found for less than thirty minutes a day."

Many female athletes run to gain strength and endurance for other sports. Sun-tanned Carla Wittenberg, twenty, from Laguna Beach, California, runs regularly to keep in shape for the University of Colorado's varsity tennis team. "Running up and down the steps of the football stadium is also great for my footwork," she declares. "If it doesn't kill me first!"

Carla's teammate, Frances Chase, of Santa Monica, California, finds another plus in running. "It helps me work out my problems," says the tall, dark-haired senior. "Many times when something is bothering me I just go out and run. Often the perfect solution will pop into my head like a light bulb turning on. Then I wonder, Why didn't I think of that before?"

Karen Orr, a young teacher, enjoys her pre-school run because it provides the only time in the day she has strictly for herself. She expresses the feelings of many runners: "Nobody is judging me; nobody is grading me on how far I run. Nobody even cares. I do this strictly for my own satisfaction."

Why do most runners report "feeling good" or being "completely happy" during a run? It may be because of norepinephrine. This hormone is found in high levels in the bloodstreams of those who exercise rhythmically and vigorously for long periods of time. Scientists do not yet know whether this hormone is the cause of "runner's high" or the result. But they do know the two are connected in some intriguing way.

All those happy runners achieve distances and speeds that vary as much as their sizes and shapes. Their motivations range from "I want to get rid of my flab" to "I want to compete in the Olympics."

But they all share one common attitude. As Kim Gallagher puts it, "When I run, I feel good!"

2. Improving

A good athletic performance is like the frosting on a birthday cake in a bakery window. It is beautiful to see, but few people really know what lies underneath.

When a gymnast like Michelle Dean or Debbi Fuhrman does a back handspring on a balance beam, for instance, it looks easy. But how many people know that they have spent hours, weeks, months—even years—improving their skills?

Michelle Dean, twelve, of Doraville, Georgia, spends at least thirteen hours every week working out in a gym. Then at night she does 150 sit-ups, lifts weights, rides a bicycle, and jogs.

She has faithfully kept to this schedule for the past two years. She tried out three different coaches and programs before she found one that suited her, Gym Elite.

Most of the friends who started tumbling with her have dropped out, but Michelle persists. While cheerleading may be a secondary activity, she is dedicated to gymnastics.

She ticks off her goals: "I want to work up to a higher class . . . I want to enter USGF (United States Gymnastics Federation) competition soon . . . I want to go as far as I can."

Michelle has just recently qualified as a Class III gymnast. She believes she has made her greatest improvement in the last three months. Why?

"I was inspired by an older girl—a Class I gymnast," she reveals. "I watched her do back tucks on the high beam. It was

NISSEN

so beautiful. I decided I want to be as good as she is. But I know I have to work at it."

The inspiration of other girls in classes often spurs young gymnasts to improve. Many girls, like Michelle, first begin gymnastics in a local Y class. Gymnastics has also become increasingly popular as a high school intramural sport. But most public schools lack space, equipment, experienced coaches, and time to develop girls' gymnastic skills.

As they advance, therefore, most girls seek coaching in one of the 3,800 private gymnastic schools scattered across the country. Hourly group rates may range from $3.75 to $10; private rates go up to $30.

The next step toward improvement may be to attend a summer camp. "Summer camp" for most old-timers brings back memories of hiking along tree-lined trails, swimming in weed-bottomed ponds, and whispering secrets in mosquito-ridden tents.

Camps featuring these activities still do exist. But today the emphasis is on specialty camps—for weight reduction, dramatics, orchestra, modern dance, travel, speech therapy, college touring, survival training, academics, or sports.

For girls, the sports boom has produced private camps specializing in tennis, golf, horseback riding, skiing, swimming and diving, sailing, soccer, basketball, hockey, figure skating, and gymnastics.

The AAU conducts a developmental camp program in each of the seventeen sports included in the Junior Olympics. The AAU or the governing body of each sport (as listed at the back of this book) can provide information on the programs.

How can one choose a good sports camp? By writing for brochures from camps advertising in sports magazines, by asking local coaches for recommendations, or by quizzing former campers. The Advisory Council for Camps offers a free service for locating suitable camps for children and teenagers.

"I want to go as far as I can in gymnastics," says Michelle Dean

Richard Brister

Sports camps are no longer limited to summer. They may also run during Christmas or spring vacation.

Camps offer an opportunity to develop athletic skills in a concentrated period. They provide accessible facilities, experienced coaches, and a wide selection of partners, teammates, and opponents for practice and competition.

For a week or a month or a summer, there are no distractions of homework, traveling long distances, or searching for someone to play with. Everything is right there. Many camps use the excellent facilities of colleges or prep schools. Campers often stay in air-conditioned dormitories—a far cry from those rain-soaked tents. But they work hard.

A session of the Parkette Gymnastic Camp, for example, resembles a nine-ring circus, but grim determination fills the air. On a humid summer day, two hundred girls, dressed in colorful leotards, gym shorts, or bodysuits, are energetically working out at the Allentown College gymnasium.

> Some race full tilt toward a padded vaulting horse, jump on a springboard, and somersault over. Others swing rhythmically on the uneven parallel bars, execute arrow-straight handstands, and drop lightly to the floor.
>
> A nervous, pony-tailed ten-year-old is being cheered on by her friends to perform two unassisted back flips on a balance beam. They applaud loudly when she succeeds.
>
> A coach helps the tumbling group learn new maneuvers by "spotting" (or hoisting) them at difficult points. His hand tangles in the pocket of one girl's shorts and they both fall to the floor laughing.

Seven hours a day for one, two, or three weeks the campers receive instruction and practice their skills. At night they see

Like every young gymnast, Michelle Dean dreams of being the American answer to Olga and Nadia
Richard Brister

films of national competitions or watch exhibitions by the staff and top gymnasts. Sometimes they perform in a show themselves. They usually have little time or strength left over for the swimming, volleyball, or tennis that the camp also offers.

They range in ability from almost beginners to some of the top gymnasts in the country. Mixed in with the campers are members of the Parkette Gymnastic Team, thirty-three girls who train year-round at the Lehigh Valley Gymnastic Training Center and compete nationally.

One of the Parkettes is Debbi Fuhrman, a five-foot tall, 81-pound sixteen-year-old who has reached the top or "elite" class of gymnasts. She is dressed in a red sleeveless bodysuit, with her curly brown hair pulled back in a ponytail. Debbi begins her day strengthening her arms and legs by lifting weights on the Universal Gym equipment.

"I have a lot of catching up to do," Debbi says between sit-ups and arm lifts. "I have to get back in shape to compete with girls who have been training every day for the past year." The structured schedule of the camp is exactly what she wants and needs right now, because she recently took a year off from gymnastics to concentrate on academics.

"I knew that eleventh grade is a model year for college," she explains. "I figured college and my whole life were more important than one year in gymnastics. I had to get my schoolwork in. But as a result, I'm weak," she adds, lifting more weights with her feet.

Debbi's dilemma is one that faces many athletes:

How can I practice and still do my schoolwork?

How can I do my schoolwork and still practice?

To resolve this dilemma, they may have to try different approaches. What works for one may not work for another, and vice versa.

During her six years as a gymnast, Debbi has tried a variety of solutions. Her first years were the easiest, because the Y where she began and the private gym where she later received coaching were less than an hour from her Long Island home.

Years of practice contribute to Debbi Fuhrman's "elite" performance

Times—Chronicle

When she moved with her family to Jenkintown, Pennsylvania, she was invited to train with a world-famous coach on a newly forming team. She could live at home and practice after school and on weekends. But soon after, unfortunately, the coach died. The team dissolved and no other top coach was available nearby.

Then at fourteen, Debbi left home to attend a special gymnastic school in another state. One of twelve girls living in a dormitory, Debbi studied major subjects in a nearby private school that was geared to the gymnasts' schedules. She attended classes from 8 A.M. to noon weekdays and then worked out in the gym for six hours.

"But dorm life was really chaotic," she remembers. "And I missed my family." She also felt that the scholastic work was not up to standard. So after a year she sought another arrangement in which both academics and gymnastics would be excellent.

The coaching at the Lehigh Valley Gymnastic Training Center met her gymnastic needs, so she went to live with an aunt, who fortunately lived in the same town. She then enrolled in the local public high school. But the school, which did not have a gymnastic team of its own, was unwilling to make many allowances for her practice schedule or the time missed for traveling to competitions.

A full course of studies, five hours in the gym, and a great deal of homework left her dropping exhausted into bed at 1 A.M., only to rise again at 6:30 A.M. to begin all over.

Within two months she realized that the load was too heavy to carry. She returned home, attended the small local high school (which did not field a gymnastic team), and devoted herself to her studies. Her gymnastic training was limited to Saturdays and as much jogging and exercising as she could do on her own. Now, academically, she is in good shape, but gymnastically, "not so good." She feels as if she is riding a seesaw.

Still, many girls do manage to balance schoolwork with athletics. How do they do it?

"They are lucky enough to have an understanding and cooperative school system," answers Parkette director, Bill Strauss, who is a teacher himself. "Coaches have to go to administrations and plead for special programs for the girls. The parents have to fight for them, too, and often they face a lot of resistance."

Today, school systems in the United States are just beginning to recognize the value of adjusting their regulations to allow dedicated athletes to train and compete in sports outside their own school programs. From following Olympic and other international events, some now realize that top champions are produced by countries in which athletes are given special assistance and encouragement.

America may not be willing to operate as the U.S.S.R. and several other countries do, selecting promising athletes at a very young age, training them intensively, and subsidizing all their expenses. But individual teachers, schools, and administrations can allow lighter course loads, advance homework assignments, makeup work, and private tutoring. At the very least, for dedicated athletes they can waive the mandatory gym rule!

Media coverage of the Olympics and other world-class sports events has certainly increased the value of women's sports in the eyes of millions of Americans, not just school administrators. The crowd-pleasing Olga Korbut became an international star overnight in the 1972 Munich Olympics. And the more withdrawn, but technically perfect, Nadia Comaneci followed in 1976. Spectators the world over realized that female athletes were worth watching.

Every girl pirouetting, vaulting, and somersaulting in a gymnasium today is secretly yearning to be the U.S. answer to Olga and Nadia.

In competition, each girl must perform in four events—balance beam, vaulting, bars, and floor exercise (which is a combination of tumbling and dance movements). Judging is based on form, flexibility, control, and difficulty of skills. ROV—risk, originality, and virtuosity—also counts for critical points.

Scoring is basically a deductive process, beginning with a perfect 10.0 score. Points are subtracted for such things as landing improperly, exceeding the time allowance, not performing a required move, or going outside the designated floor exercise area.

Girls compete within their own age groups (15 and up, 12–14, 10–11) and work their way up through four levels: Class IV, Class III, Class II, and Class I. At the top is elite class, which has two age groupings, 12–14 and 15 and up. Only about fifty girls in the United States qualify for this group.

By scoring a certain point average in local meets, a gymnast qualifies to enter state meets. She then progresses to regional, sectional, and national meets. The top twenty U.S. champions compete in the World Game Final Trials for six positions, one alternate and three "alternate alternate" spots.

Trials to qualify for the Olympic team begin in April of the Olympic year for the summer games. The United States Gymnastics Federation governs qualifying systems and training programs for the United States Olympic Committee (USOC).

Each of the thirty-two Olympic sports is governed by a specific organization, which is a member of the USOC. Each organization sets its own standards for qualification.

Women's teams include archery, athletics (track and field), basketball, canoeing and kayaking, diving, fencing, field hockey, figure skating, gymnastics, luge, rowing, skiing (alpine and nordic), speed skating, swimming, team handball, and volleyball. Women also participate in mixed equestrian, shooting, and yachting teams.

In addition, the Pan-American Games include women's teams in baseball, roller skating, softball, synchronized swimming, and tennis.

For information about Olympic team selection, one should contact the member organization that governs her sport (as listed at the back of this book). Local and national key persons are listed in the *Directory of Member Organizations,* which is available from the United States Olympic Committee, Training Center-Colorado Springs, 1776 East Boulder Street, Colorado Springs, CO 80909.

The Olympics, however, come only once every four years. And sometimes, as in 1980, they are boycotted by some countries. But every year, a few lucky athletes are invited to national and international competitions.

"Travel opportunities are among the biggest benefits the gymnasts receive," says Parkette director and coach, Donna Strauss. Donna accompanies her team members on many trips. "The girls get to sightsee and meet people in other countries. They also get to see the outstanding gymnastic facilities around the world."

For top gymnasts, invitations to international competitions come through the USGF. The host country provides food, lodging, and transportation within its boundaries. The USGF may provide half or all of the airfare to the meet.

Who pays the rest? Individual families or the club that the gymnast represents. The Parkette Team, for example, raises money through gymnastic exhibitions, souvenir programs, and candy sales. They even raised $2,000 from a Cartwheelathon, when sponsors donated a dime for each cartwheel or a quarter for a back handspring.

One of the Strausses' full-time professional coaches is Robin Bleamer Netwall, who was once their student. Robin especially enjoys teaching pink-suited three- to five-year-olds in kindergym. She does not need to be a certified instructor, because certification is not yet mandated.

In addition to worldwide travel, Robin feels that college scholarships can be important benefits to gymnasts. "They don't even need to be top-ranked," she explains. "Some of the smaller colleges are looking for Class II gymnasts." In 1978–79, 95 American colleges offered financial aid and 151 more offered gymnastic programs without financial aid.

International travel, scholarships, coaching jobs, and Olympic gold medals may seem very distant goals to a petite ponytailed girl doing back flips at a summer camp. Still, if she can develop flexibility, grace, strength, jumping power, body awareness, and a certain amount of fearlessness, she may one day achieve those goals.

On this hot and humid summer day, Debbi Fuhrman is working hard toward her own personal goals. She advises other girls: "You just have to try gymnastics. If you like it, you keep at it." Then she gracefully executes an intricate series of aerial maneuvers. She raises her arms high in a victor's salute.

3. Finding the Right Coach

Finding the right coach may be even trickier than choosing the right family dog. Some people like cocker spaniels; others like German shepherds.

Once a girl has chosen a sport she likes, learned the basic skills, and entered a few local competitions, she may ask herself, "Do I need a coach?"

What about swimming, for example, when the object of a race is simply to get from one end of the pool to the other faster than anyone else? Does a swimmer really need a special coach to help her become a winner?

"Yes!" answer swimmers from places as far apart as Palo Alto, California, Lincoln, Nebraska, and Wayne, Pennsylvania. "I know I wouldn't be where I am today without my coach!"

Today, backstroker Libby Kinkead is receiving instructions from her coach at an indoor pool near her Wayne, Pennsylvania, home. At fourteen, Libby is preparing for the Nationals in Florida next week. She has already won a bronze medal at the Pan-American Games to add to her many trophies. And she has qualified for the Olympic Trials.

A coach first influenced Libby when she was just six years old. Her voice came over the loudspeaker at Libby's local swim club: "We need more members for the swim team. Sign up at the pool desk right away!"

Libby might still be splashing around in the pool playing "Marco Polo" with her friends if she had not listened to that coach. Instead, she spent several summers learning the basics and competing in area swim meets with the team. Then, at eleven, she progressed to indoor swimming at the local Y.

"I loved the coaches there and hated to leave them," remembers brown-haired Libby. But, at fourteen, she realized she needed something more in the way of coaching. She and her family investigated the philosophies and programs of several coaches until they found the right one. The disciplined training program of Olympic coach George Haines at the nearby Foxcatcher Swim Club seemed exactly right for her.

But Libby faced stiff competition even to get into that program. It was held at an Olympic-sized indoor pool which millionaire John du Pont had built on his Newtown Square estate to provide Eastern swimmers a place to develop into champions. And Mr. du Pont had hired George Haines away from California, where for many years he had successfully coached Santa Clara High School and UCLA teams, as well as five Olympic teams. Libby felt herself very lucky when she was chosen for that program.

Swimmers, as well as athletes in other sports, often travel thousands of miles to train with a certain coach.

For example, Anne Lambert, a blond sixteen-year-old breaststroker, has come all the way from Palo Alto, California, to train with George Haines. She is living with the Kinkeads this summer, but her whole family plans to move East this fall to be with her while she trains for the Olympics.

Coaching is so important to fifteen-year-old Lisa McClain, who specializes in the individual medley, that she once persuaded her family to move from the East Coast to the West Coast to get top coaching for her. Once there, however, she found the workouts too easy for her liking. So she and her very supportive family again moved bag and baggage back East so she could train with George.

What makes one coach so outstanding that whole families will move clear across the country for him?

"He really understands each person," Anne says. "He gets the best out of you and he puts you in top competitions."

"He works you hard," adds Lisa, "and I need that."

"He doesn't yell at you," Libby contributes. "I couldn't handle it if a coach yelled at me all the time. With George, if you work hard and come to all the practices, you can get along really well with him. It's a two-way street."

Libby Kinkead is the kind of swimmer George likes to coach. "Libby has solid ability," he declares, out of her hearing. "And she is a hard worker. She doesn't let a defeat get under her skin; she accepts the losses along with the wins. She has a good attitude."

Just what is "a good attitude" for a swimmer? "Dedication, willingness to work," George says thoughtfully. "Loyalty—putting herself in the coach's hands, doing what he says. Going along with training away from the pool, not being swayed by peers." He is very strict about drinking and marijuana smoking. "I'll drop anyone if I find out—I don't care if it's my top swimmer!"

Coach Haines recommends eight or nine hours of sleep nightly and three good meals a day plus vitamins. "I guess a certain amount of junk food is okay," he adds. "After all, a swimmer burns up 5,000 to 6,000 calories a day. But I keep track of their weight and if they gain, I get after them. Or I get Janie after them."

He points to his assistant coach, Janie Tyler, who was a gold medal winner in the '68 and '72 Olympics. Janie understands swimming from both the participant's and the coach's points of view. After she ended her own competitive career, she coached the women's team at the University of Tennessee. Now, in addition to the summer Foxcatcher program, she coaches the Princeton University women's team during the academic year.

"I like the challenge of helping other swimmers improve," she says. "Swimming gets in your blood—you never lose the thrill of competing and winning!"

Janie believes that coaching jobs for women are now beginning to open up. "Clubs, schools, and colleges are actively looking for women," she says. "It's partly because of Title IX —so many more girls are proving themselves in all sports now." Title IX of the Education Amendments Act, passed by

"I couldn't handle it if a coach yelled at me all the time,"
says backstroker Libby Kinkead

Suburban and Wayne Times

Congress in 1972, guarantees girls equal opportunities with boys in all areas, including sports in federally funded schools.

In order to make the transition from participant to coach, Janie observed many different coaches. In her early years as a coach, she had difficulty in keeping a distance between herself and her swimmers, because she was so near their age. Now, at the ripe old age of twenty-seven, she finds that problem nearly gone—at times she feels it is important to be a friend without being too close. "I want their respect first," she declares.

Often the swimmers come to Janie for advice, sometimes about boyfriends or family problems. During a break in the practice, one young woman asks a typical question about colleges: "I want a place that has good swimming, but is good for academics, too. What do you think about this one?"

Janie gives her approval to the academic reputation of the college and adds, "I know the coach—you'll like her." But then she cautions, "Try to go to visit a few colleges and talk to the coaches. You don't want to jump in too quickly."

Halfway across the country in Lincoln, Nebraska, another nationally ranked swimmer, Barb Harris, twenty, shares this cautious philosophy.

"I have been very careful about choosing a coach as well as a college," says this 5'8½", 137-pound sprinter. "I went through three or four coaches in clubs and high school trying to find the right one for me."

What does Barb look for? "Someone with experience, of course," she answers. "But also someone who will listen to my ideas. After swimming for thirteen years, I know a lot about what will work for me. We both have to be able to compromise."

Barb's swimming record certainly made her attractive to many coaches. By fourteen, she had won three gold medals and a silver in the Junior Olympics. Later, she placed three times in the top eight of the Senior Nationals in the freestyle and butterfly.

She can be an inspiration to swimmers from all parts of the country. She proves that one does not have to come from the "power" areas of swimming (the East and West Coasts). One does not need year-round sunshine or even a millionaire's swimming pool in order to become a champion.

Barb comes from a cold, flat, windswept Midwestern city. At five o'clock in the morning, all through the winters, she would leave her warm house and get into a cold car to go to swim practice. "Often it was ten degrees below zero," she remembers with a shiver. "And with the wind-chill factor, a lot colder

Swimmers burn 5,000 to 6,000 calories a day
Montgomery Newspapers

than that." Later, her hair would still be wet as she left practice and headed for a full day of school.

But her grit and determination brought rewards. When the time came to choose a college, Barb received scholarship offers from ten colleges in her area plus several top-ranked universities. Some of them I had to look up in an atlas," she laughs, "because I had hardly ever been out of Nebraska." Her mother helped her do research on the Top Ten.

Then Barb sat down with a piece of paper and made a chart listing the colleges and her three most important criteria, which were: academics, the team, and the coach. "The University of North Carolina came out overwhelmingly on top for my needs," she remembers.

The women's swim team of UNC at Chapel Hill had ranked in the Top Ten for five years. So far, the coach, Frank Comfort, had only communicated with Barb through a letter. But then she had a chance to meet him at a national meet. "I knew right away he was the type of coach I was looking for," she says

"I look for a coach who will listen to my ideas," says Barb Harris. "We both have to compromise"

enthusiastically. Now in her second year at UNC, Barb knows she made the right decision.

That decision made Coach Comfort happy, too. Barb is just the kind of swimmer he looks for. Because he can only choose five to ten swimmers each year, he is very specific about what qualities he wants.

"First," he declares, "I look for a young woman who is very concerned about her academic future. Second, I want someone who can say please and thank you with ease, who is well-mannered, who comes from a good, stable family background with support and love.

"Third, she must have a good somatic (body) type. I steer clear of someone who will get fat or who has a history of injuries. And fourth, I look for sheer athletic performance—the time records tell the story."

In other sports as well as swimming, a sought-after athlete will have been a "top fish" in her home area. But when she gets to the college level, she may only be No. 15 on the team. "She has to be a well-adjusted person," Coach Comfort believes. "She has to relate well to other people."

The relationship between coach and athlete is usually an intensely personal and long-lasting one. No two relationships are alike. Sometimes both parties must make adjustments and compromises. The most important factor, however, is that they share the same primary goal—reaching the athlete's full potential.

To achieve that potential, most athletes need the stimulation of stiff competition. Part of the coach's job is to arrange that competition. Since many girls and their families are unfamiliar at first with competitive circuits and levels, the coach must advise them on schedules, applications, transportation, and even finances.

Finances are bound to come into the athletic picture. Public funds currently provide free or low-cost coaching in municipal clinics, elementary after-school sports clubs, and high school teams. However, increased costs and budget-tightening could cause these programs to be limited or even eliminated.

Athletes who need special facilities, such as indoor swim-

Barb Harris braved many cold Nebraska mornings to attend swim practice

ming pools, golf courses, or gymnastic equipment, must be prepared to pay the extra fees for them.

Transportation to competitions must often be paid for by participants' families or by organizations' fund-raising projects. Clothing and equipment, especially in individual sports like tennis or golf, must also be provided by the athlete.

Private coaching in athletics, just as in music or art, is always paid for by the individual. Prices can vary from sport to sport, or even within a sport, according to the quality. Tennis lessons, for example, can range from $4 per hour with an accomplished teenaged teacher to $50 with a nationally known professional.

Each person must decide whether the expense of special coaching is worth the rewards. The athlete's entire family must sometimes make sacrifices in order to provide the coach, school, or program best suited to her development.

Most of the girls interviewed have had more than one coach; many have had several. A change of coach may be necessary because coach or athlete moves away, or because of a personality conflict, or because the athlete progresses beyond the coach's ability. Even girls lucky enough to have a talented parent for an initial coach may eventually need to move on to another.

Circumstances sometimes make the change friendly and casual, but other times it can be "sticky" or even traumatic. For example, within a year after Libby Kinkead was interviewed, the United States boycotted the Summer Olympics in Moscow. Foxcatcher Swim Club closed, George Haines moved back to California, and Libby had to find another coach. The whole situation was traumatic for her. But, on the bright side, she made a goodwill tour of China as a member of an honorary Olympic team.

Each athlete must decide what she wants and needs in a coach. One girl may seek the friendly encouragement of a cocker spaniel type; another seeks the stern discipline of a German shepherd sort. The choice is up to her.

However, in order to make the relationship successful, each athlete must bring to it the eagerness of a young dog to learn new tricks.

4. Climbing the Ladder

Competitive sportswomen like to measure their success. They like to know how their performances rate with other sportswomen. And they try to move onward and upward.

Racquet sports provide a ladder to climb. And a player knows on which rung she stands at any given time.

A racquet player is not like a basketball player, for instance, for whom much depends on teammates and opponents. A racquet player, except when supported by a doubles partner, must climb or slip on that ladder alone.

Every playing moment, she knows exactly how she compares to her opponent, because each point of each game of each set of each match is scored.

She also knows how she compares with other players. On a school or club team, her performance is recorded on a "ladder," which is a poster or plaque with movable names. She advances up that ladder by challenging and defeating players listed above her, while defending her position from those below.

If she plays tournaments, she earns a ranking, which is a numerical standing tabulated from her wins and losses. Then she knows how she compares with players in her district, state, region, nation, and even the world.

Kathy Jordan is an expert ladder climber. In July 1979, on a ladder that includes all the female tennis players in the world, Kathy stands on the fourteenth rung—from the top.

But now on a warm morning in the living room of her family's home in King of Prussia, Pennsylvania, she looks like any other teenager. Her jean-clad legs sprawl over the arm of an easy chair. A friendly smile lights her face.

Can this be the same young woman the papers called "aggressive" and "dominant" and "hard-slugging" when she defeated the world's fifth-ranked player, Tracy Austin? Where is that fierce scowl of concentration she usually wears on the tennis court? Only the lily-white bare feet, contrasting with a golden tan, give her away as a veteran tennis player.

Though only nineteen, Kathy certainly is a veteran. For twelve straight years, ever since she was seven, she has been playing tennis tournaments. She has competed indoors and out; on clay, composition, grass, and hard courts; in winter, spring, summer, and fall. She has had little time to brood over defeats or exult over victories, for she always had another match coming up.

Doesn't the constant pressure get to her? Doesn't she "burn out"?

"No," says the Stanford University sophomore thoughtfully. "Because I do just what I'm doing now—I take time off, maybe a week or a month. I have fun with my friends, play basketball, catch up on my studies, read, or just listen to music. And I don't even pick up a racquet."

This particular layoff comes right after her return from Wimbledon, England, where she played in the tennis world's most prestigious tournament. Her winning streak was broken only by third-seeded Evonne Goolagong Cawley in a thrilling three-set, two tie-breaker match.

(Little does she know that within a year she will capture the Wimbledon doubles trophy with Texan Anne Smith. Or that she will defeat Evonne in straight sets in the Canadian Open.)

Right now Kathy, whose curly reddish-brown hair is styled much in the fashion of her Australian opponent, is still reliving the match.

"I had a lot of chances," she recalls. "I just wish I could have taken advantage of more of them!" She admits that she does not like to lose. She is often bothered with regrets and disap-

Kathy Jordan's eye never leaves the ball during her back-
hand stroke

Robert Beyers

pointment after losing an important match.

"But after a while, I start to think about other things. I begin
working toward the next tournament," she adds with a broad
grin.

Kathy has scored many more victories than defeats in her

46

career. Glittering silver trophies—huge trays, bowls, and pitchers—decorate her living room as proof.

"Many of these belong to my sister, Barbara," she replies modestly when questioned about them. "And one of my favorites we won together." She displays a large walnut and copper plaque topped by the AIAW (Association for Intercollegiate Athletics for Women) symbol.

In 1978, when Kathy was a freshman and Barbara was a junior at Stanford University in California, the sisters joined forces as a doubles team. In the season's end tournament, they defeated doubles teams from top-ranked colleges all over the country and won the plaque.

"That was one of the best times of my life!" Kathy exclaims. "All of us from Stanford were a team. We were all rooting for each other and we played hard to keep from letting the others down. Afterward we had a big party. It was great!"

Barbara, who is two and a half years older, has always been an inspiration and example for Kathy. As singles players at Upper Merion High School, they defeated every opponent. Playing the tournament circuits, they both achieved outstanding records. ("I was a late bloomer," Kathy says. "I began doing well nationally at about sixteen.")

Then Barbara won a full scholarship to Stanford and Kathy followed in her footsteps two years later. Barbara was graduated in January and turned professional.

Has there been rivalry between the two? "No!" declares Kathy emphatically. "We were always in different age groups, so we never had to compete against each other." Then she adds with a grin, "Besides, it's a great asset to have a practice partner right in your own family!"

Kathy has another great asset in her own family—her father, Bob Jordan, who is her coach. Mr. Jordan was not a professional when he began teaching his little daughters the strokes and strategies of tennis. Due to his interest in their progress, however, he became a leading figure in the Philadelphia Gold Cup Program for junior development as well as the Middle States Tennis Association. Now that both his daughters are away, he has built a tennis court on his property and started a professional training program for other young tournament players.

Leading the cheering section is her mother, Virginia, who aspires only to play friendly ladies' doubles matches at her local club. Over the years, however, Mrs. Jordan has driven her daughters thousands of miles to hundreds of tournaments and run untold tons of tennis whites through her washing machine. Perhaps mothers like her should be given more credit for their part in their offspring's success.

Mrs. Jordan was interviewed after Kathy, then ranked No. 28, had upset Tracy Austin in front of an enthusiastic home-town audience at the Avon Futures Championships. Mrs. Jor-

"All of us from Stanford were a team," Kathy Jordan *(left)* remembers. "We were rooting for each other"

Robert Beyers

dan told reporters that neither Kathy nor Barbara was pushed toward success in tennis.

"It's their life," she declared. "They're the ones who put in all the work on it."

At that time, a very important decision was coming up in Kathy's life—to turn pro or not to turn pro, that was the question. If she turned pro, she could no longer play for the top-ranked Stanford team and she would forfeit her scholarship. But there was the lure of all that prize money. The decision was up to her and her alone.

Kathy put the decision off until June 1979 to see how well she did in the AIAW tournament. In the meantime, the money she would have won had she not retained her amateur standing amounted to about $27,000.

The AIAW tournament came. She won both the singles and the doubles. She felt she had done everything she could do in college tennis. So she turned professional.

"It is the next logical step in sequence," she states simply. "It is time to go on."

Not every girl has a father for a coach and a sister for a practice partner, nor the ability and will to win of Kathy Jordan. Not every girl aspires to more than a fun-filled game with friends.

But for every girl who has enough competitive spirit to want to climb the tennis ladder, there are certain steps to follow. These steps are similar in the other racquet sports—racquetball, paddle, platform tennis, and squash—although the governing organizations set up their own regulations.

The first step, of course, is to learn the game. Local parks, schools, private clubs, and Y's offer series of group lessons or clinics. Tennis camps, both day and overnight, provide concentrated instruction and court time. (*Tennis USA* publishes a directory of camps in the January issue each year.) Players who have attended the camps or clinics can offer valuable advice about them.

For intermediate and advanced players, some areas offer junior development programs on a free or cost-sharing basis. These programs are by invitation only to those who have

earned a local ranking or shown promise in other programs.
Later, private coaching may seem necessary for further advancement. A private coach can be objective about the player and can provide guidance and strategy as well as technical stroke production.

Aggressive play made Kathy Jordan winner of both singles and doubles in the 1979 AIAW Championships

Robert Beyers

Some ambitious players even seek full-time instruction far away from home. For example, Carling Bassett, twelve, left her family in Toronto, Canada, to attend the Nick Bollettieri Tennis Academy in Longboat Key, Florida.

"Only by living, eating, and sleeping tennis can a person expect to excel in today's competitive game," is the philosophy instilled in Carling and sixty other students at the academy.

"I don't have much time for sunbathing on the beach," Carling says with a flick of her long blond ponytail. "And I only go home twice a year. I go to tennis camp in Wisconsin in the summer.

"But it's worth it." For emphasis, she grunts with the effort of a smashing serve. As a result of her year-and-a-half work at the academy, she is now ranked No. 1 in Florida in her age group.

From September to June, Carling lives in a motel-dormitory with other students and instructors from all over America and other countries. Every morning she attends academic classes at a private school nearby. Her afternoon program consists of drilling and supervised play at the courts of the Colony Beach and Tennis Resort, followed by strengthening and stretching exercises, foot drills, agility drills, and long-distance running on the beach.

The instructors do not believe in coddling their blossoming stars, however. Coach Donna Roberts, from New Orleans, rifles a shopping-cartful of balls at Carling.

"Okay, you turkey, move your feet!" Donna shouts. Carling responds by returning a string of perfect volleys from all parts of the court.

"I think Carling will be one of our top stars," Donna says privately. "She's willing to work at her game . . . and she loves to 'kill'!"

Boarding schools specializing in a variety of sports are being founded today. They are expensive. The Bollettieri Tennis Academy charges about $1,000 a month for room, board, lessons, and transportation. Academic school costs are extra. But

Carling Bassett *(right)* practices serves under the watchful eye of instructor Donna Roberts

Gail Andersen Myers

for those willing to stand the expense, the separation from home, and the day-and-night dedication, the possible benefits are summer employment, a college scholarship, a vocation as a teaching professional or playing professional, as well as a lifetime of enjoyment.

To play in tournaments, every player must be a member of the United States Tennis Association. The USTA, which is the official governing body of tennis, is divided geographically into seventeen active sectional associations and fifty districts across the country.

A membership form may be obtained by writing: USTA, 51 East 42d Street, New York, NY 10017. A yearly junior membership (under 21) includes a subscription to the informative magazine *Tennis World* and the newspaper *Tennis USA.*

When joining USTA, a player should ask for the mailing address of the section in which she lives. Next she should write to that section for a copy of the annual yearbook, which lists the names of local leaders to contact. The yearbook lists tournament schedules for the coming year, player rankings from the previous year, special awards, and important ranking regulations.

The tournament schedule includes the dates, events (for boys or girls, singles, doubles, mixed doubles), age groups (12 and under, 13–14, 15–16, 17–18, 19–21), location, entrant fees, and addresses to write for entry forms.

Armed with a calendar and a map, a player may then plot out which tournaments can be reached by car or public transportation. Overnight housing in local homes is sometimes available. She should then write for the appropriate entry forms and be careful to return them before the closing date. Sometimes she will be informed of her first match time; sometimes she must contact the sponsor the night before the match.

The first year, competing in tournaments can be rather lonely and discouraging. A girl may feel like "cannon fodder" when she frequently meets top-seeded players in early rounds. The luck of the draw usually improves with time, experience, and ranking, however.

A doubles partner can make the experience more fun. Companionship and transportation-sharing can be equally as important as strong support on the court. Having a regular doubles partner is not absolutely necessary, though. One can often pick up a partner at the tournament. Since the doubles events do not usually start until the second or third day, a player can often team up with another girl who has not been eliminated in the singles.

As the season progresses, the same faces begin to appear at various tournaments. Warm off-court friendships develop even among fierce on-court competitors.

After playing in several tournaments and sending a list of results to the section headquarters, a player receives a ranking for the season—October 1 to September 30 in tennis—for her district or section, or the United States for top players. Even close losses can boost the ranking.

Why get a ranking? Eve Kraft, director of the USTA Education and Research Center in Princeton, New Jersey, replies, "A ranking is important because this is a way that your district, section, and eventually, the national junior development committee get to know you as one of their better players.

"A junior who wants to reach the top should play as many local, state, and regional sanctioned tournaments as possible. Through these sanctioned tournaments in the sectional associations, highly ranked juniors eventually earn the opportunity to attend special training camps and become eligible for Junior Wightman Cup (for girls) or Junior Davis Cup (for boys) and qualify to compete nationally."

Each district association selects the best six or eight players to form the Junior Wightman teams. The top fifteen girls in the United States are chosen for the national Junior Federation Cup Team. The team's transportation, entry fees, food, and lodging are provided by the USTA. During training camp and the six- or seven-week tour, these players are continually given coaching by a traveling coach or assistant.

Besides being selected for national team play, many top-ranked juniors compete on the national circuit as individuals. This stage of junior activity is the most costly one, but those who qualify usually receive some financial assistance from their respective sections.

Some highly ranked players, like Kathy Jordan, choose to turn professional. They must realize that the pro circuit is financially grim for those who do not make the top few dozen slots. Unless a generous sponsor can be found, the backing of personal funds is usually necessary.

For those who feel qualified and ready to tackle the pro circuit, the USTA provides many fine opportunities. These include the Futures circuit for women and an expanding number of satellite events. Further information about these tournaments may be obtained from the USTA director of women's tennis or the Women's Tennis Association.

The purses get bigger every year:

TOTAL WOMEN'S TENNIS PURSES WORLDWIDE

1973	1978	1979	1980
$1,500,000	$5,500,000	$7,500,000	$9,100,000

Hitting buckets of balls to perfect a serve suddenly seems more appealing!

According to the USTA, prize money for the U.S. Open Championships, the richest tournament in the world, has also jumped dramatically:

U.S. OPEN CHAMPIONSHIPS

	1970	1975	1980
Women's Singles total purse	$15,425	$49,700	$225,304
Women's Singles winner's share	$7,500	$25,000	$46,000
Women's Doubles total purse	$3,750	$10,350	$58,770
Women's Doubles Team winners' share	$2,000	$4,500	$18,500

Even hitting for hours against a backboard begins to look worthwhile.

In 1973, proportionally speaking, women began receiving pay equal to men in the U.S. Open. (There were more men than women in the draw.) In 1979, for the first time in the U.S. Open, the women's winner's share was the same amount as the men's.

In the racquet sports, a girl has several choices. She can

choose to climb only high enough to play a casual game with her friends, to enjoy the fresh air, the exercise, and the fun. Or she can choose to teach others. Or, like Kathy Jordan and Carling Bassett, she can choose to fight her way upward through amateur and professional competition.

5. Getting a Scholarship

Sports can be a girl's ticket to college today. For many who could not afford it otherwise, it is the only ticket to college. For others, an athletic scholarship helps lighten the financial burden of education.

In 1973, not one college offered women athletic scholarships. By 1978, 450 colleges did. In 1980, 700 colleges offered women ten thousand scholarships—worth more than $7,000,000—in twenty-two sports. And those numbers will continue to increase every year.

But these scholarships do not arrive on a silver platter. Good athletes and superstars alike must do careful research before making decisions. They may even need to do some shrewd detective work.

Athletic scholarships are very new. Until a few years ago, there were scholarships for academic brilliance or financial need, but never for athletic ability.

Why? Because the Association for Intercollegiate Athletics for Women (AIAW) had forbidden athletic scholarships for women. The AIAW disliked the high-pressure recruiting tactics that had invaded men's sports. It feared that commercialism and exploitation would enter women's sports if scholarships were possible.

But in 1974, AIAW lifted the ban. It even encouraged colleges and universities to award scholarships to women. Title IX legislation and the women's liberation movement had convinced the organization that women should have an equal opportunity for financial aid.

But AIAW issued very strict rules concerning recruiting practices. For instance, a college recruiter may not contact an athlete directly. And the college may not pay her expenses while visiting the campus. With these and other rules, AIAW strives to keep recruiting fair to all.

Scholarship winners come from all kinds of places, with all sorts of backgrounds and all types of personalities. What contrasts there are, for example, between a Jeannie Gilbert and a Debbie Lytle.

> Jeannie comes from a small Midwestern town, where she attends a private girls' school.

> Debbie comes from a big Eastern city where she attends a huge public high school.

Yet despite their differences, both are dedicated to their sports and both are being rewarded by college scholarships.

At eighteen, Jeannie was nicknamed "The Best" by the local Bloomfield Hills, Michigan, newspaper after she scored 42 field hockey goals in one season. Her record made her the top scorer in the whole state of Michigan. College coaches coast to coast took notice and watched her play in national tournaments and field days. Then twenty of them contacted her about scholarships in volleyball as well as field hockey.

Jeannie is certainly not a one-sport athlete. In addition to playing center forward and goalie in field hockey, she has been an outstanding setter and hitter in volleyball, center and guard in basketball, and played pitcher, third base, and left field in softball. She was voted Kingswood School's Most Valuable Player in all four sports. And besides all that, she was an outstanding right wing in ice hockey!

"I love sports and just being out and playing," she explains. "I guess I like field hockey best because it's fun and it can be rough. I get bored easily and field hockey is a real exciting sport!"

Brown-haired Jeannie is smaller than many other players—

Jeannie Gilbert was nicknamed "The Best" after she scored 42 field hockey goals in one season

Charles Gilbert

just 5'5" and 125 pounds. But she makes up for size with her speed, agility, and aggressiveness.

"I'm an only child," she says. "But I grew up around boys —my three male cousins and the neighborhood kids. I played whatever games they played and I learned to keep up."

During the cold Michigan winters, Jeannie played goalie on a neighborhood ice hockey team. When she entered Kingswood, a small private girls' school connected with the boys' Cranford School, she saw field hockey played for the first time. It seemed like a new and exciting sport, so she tried out for the team. Her natural athletic ability helped her make the switch from the ice to the field easily.

Then every season she played whatever sport was going on. She soon became a favorite of the spectators, her teammates,

"I get bored easily, but field hockey is a real exciting sport!" says Jeannie Gilbert *(right front)*

Charles Gilbert

and her coaches as well.

When college entrance time came, all her coaches went to bat for Jeannie. They wrote glowing letters to athletic directors and coaches of many colleges.

Recommendations from coaches are extremely helpful to a girl seeking college entrance or scholarship aid. While individual wins, times, scores, or rankings can be recorded in some sports, important qualities like cooperation, dedication, and coachability cannot.

A few good words from a high school coach can often make the difference between a yes and a no from a college coach. An athlete should not be timid about asking her coaches, gym teachers, and athletic directors to write detailed letters praising her talents and personality. Those letters can affect her whole future!

Because of her coach's enthusiastic recommendation, teamed with her outstanding basketball record, Debbie Lytle can now say, "I will be the first person in my family to go to college."

Debbie can take her choice of a dozen college scholarships. At seventeen, she has the world at her fingertips—like a basketball.

But today, on a March afternoon, she has more routine things on her mind. With her teammates on the Simon Gratz High School "Lady Bulldogs" basketball team, she is practicing for the Philadelphia Public School Play-Offs next week. If they reach the finals, they will be cheered on by hundreds of spectators at the Penn Palestra. The air crackles with excitement.

Debbie is always the center of action. Dressed in bright-red shorts and a jersey emblazoned with her famous "33," she is constantly in motion.

She dribbles the ball swiftly down the court, shakes off a defending guard, looks toward the basket, and passes to an open player. Seconds later, she darts under the basket, receives the ball, and gives it an easy underhanded toss . . . swish.

Debbie has her lay-ups, long shots, and foul shots just where she wants them—in the basket. They recently gained her the best game of her career, when she scored 44 points with 20 rebounds against an arch rival.

Even the city sportswriters, who rarely get excited about women's sports, have written enthusiastically about Debbie. They call her "versatile," "electric," "queen of area high school basketball." *The Philadelphia Inquirer* even featured her as "Athlete of the Week"—no easy title to win for a woman.

Does all this attention make Debbie nervous? "I love it," she grins during a break. "I love the exposure. I like it when people see me and say, 'I know her—she's Debbie Lytle!' "

And a lot of people are saying just that, including more than fifty college basketball coaches and recruiters from all over the country. They are vying with each other, offering her scholarships (and even cars and apartments illegally) to lure her to their schools. Within the next two weeks, she must sign a "letter of intent" indicating her final choice.

But all this fame and good fortune did not happen overnight. Debbie has played hard and worked hard at her sport as far back as she can remember.

"I always competed with the boys," she smiles. "And I guess I was good enough, so the boys let me play." As early as fourth grade, she went out for girls' track and softball. And in seventh grade she discovered basketball.

Throughout junior high school basketball she was so outstanding she was called a "one-person show." Yet she longed for the balanced team play that high school would offer.

But Simon Gratz is a tough inner-city school with three thousand students. Suddenly the flamboyant youngster was hesitant and shy. In fact, she did not even attend the tryouts for the basketball team!

Coach Ina Newman remembers that time well. "I had to coax her to join. I had to convince her we needed her." Of course, Debbie finally joined. "And now she's the best player I have ever coached in my sixteen years here!" Coach Newman exclaims.

What makes Debbie so extraordinary? Is it her height? Not really, for 5'10½" is not outstanding by today's standards—one of her teammates is 6'1".

Is it her coordination and rhythm? Partly. "I love my moves," she confesses with a grin.

Is it her coaching? Could be. In addition to Coach Newman, Debbie gets a lot of help from a friend. His name is Melvin Mack (which she carefully spells out) and he is "a friend who happens to be a boy." Melvin, who is the basketball hero of

Debbie Lytle's basketball skills won her a ticket to college
Fran O'Byrne-Pelham

Debbie Lytle *(right)* plays or practices basketball seven
hours a day

Fran O'Byrne-Pelham

the local schoolyard, has been willing to practice endless hours
with Debbie.

Debbie certainly has dedication. She practices seven hours
every day, first-team practice or games, then at the schoolyard
until dark, then inside for more play or practice with the Philadelphia Belles, a local AAU team. Summers she has attended
basketball camps with leading young players from all over the
country.

And she has dreams—playing college ball with a top-ranked
team (she has chosen the University of Maryland), studying
communications, making a try for the 1984 Summer Olympics
in Los Angeles. And after that, "Well, the new Professional
Women's Basketball League should be in full swing."

But that faraway gleam in her eye is interrupted. "Let's go,
Debbie," Coach Newman says firmly. "The team needs to
practice for the play-offs."

So Debbie cheerfully trots onto the court, receives a pass from a teammate, leaps high in the air and . . . swish.

Yes, Debbie certainly has the world at her fingertips. But what about all those other sportswomen around the country who are dribbling, spiking, lobbing, cradling, and batting with dedication. Can they get financial aid, too?

About ten thousand of them will this year. At least 700 colleges and universities are now rewarding girls' high school athletic achievements with a total of $7,000,000 worth of financial aid. In this way, they are helping to reduce the costs of higher education to the student and are encouraging sports participation among young women.

The list of sports includes:

archery	lacrosse
badminton	riflery
basketball	sailing
bowling	skiing
crew	softball
cross-country	squash
fencing	swimming and diving
field hockey	synchronized swimming
golf	tennis
gymnastics	track and field
ice hockey	volleyball

With the help of parents, coaches, and guidance counselors, as well as college catalogs, a student can locate these scholarships.

In addition, two excellent directories spell out current financial aid available to women: *Women's Sports Annual Scholarship Guide* (free from the magazine or from the Women's Sports Foundation) and the *AIAW Directory.* Addresses are listed at the back of this book.

The *Women's Sports Annual Scholarship Guide* lists colleges by states, giving athletic directors' names, numbers of scholarships offered and amounts (which may vary).

The *AIAW Directory* lists its 825 member institutions alphabetically, with sports offered and availability of scholarships based on athletic ability. Then it divides into individual sports, listing schools offering them, with and without financial aid.

Whether or not she plans to seek financial aid, a student will want to know whether the colleges that interest her offer her sport. This information can save her much time in sending for and reading college catalogs. After all, what real athlete could bear to spend two to four years at a place that did not offer her favorite sport?

Certain sports are better endowed than others, but the trends probably will shift through the years. Statistics of the top six show the dramatic increases in less than ten years:

NUMBER OF COLLEGES AND UNIVERSITIES
OFFERING WOMEN ATHLETIC SCHOLARSHIPS

	1972–73	1978–79	1980–81
Basketball	0	325	595
Volleyball	0	273	491
Tennis	0	224	411
Track & field	0	151	262
Swimming & diving	0	130	193
Softball	0	125	259

At the other end of the list are sailing, squash, ice hockey, and archery. But a woman who excels in these sports should not be afraid to try for that lone scholarship. Somebody has to win it!

After finding the names of colleges that offer her sports and scholarship possibilities, a woman must ask some other important questions. The *Women's Sports Annual Scholarship Guide* suggests these thought-provoking questions that a student should ask herself and the college:

ON SCHOLARSHIP OPPORTUNITY
1. Does the school offer the best program for my academic interests?
2. Do professors allow tutoring and makeup tests when the team schedule conflicts with classes?

ON FINANCES
1. How much of the cost of tuition, fees, and room and board

does my scholarship cover, and how much must I pay?
  2. Does the school provide a written contract stating the amount, duration, and criteria for withdrawal of my scholarship? (For example, will my scholarship be renewed if I fail to make the team?)
  3. Are there any other forms of financial aid for which I am eligible?

On Competitive Conditions
  1. How many hours a week can I expect to spend in practice?
  2. What are my chances for making the first-string team?
  3. What is the length of the season and how many games or matches are there?
  4. What is the quality of the competition?
  5. May I participate in intercollegiate sports other than the one for which I have been awarded the scholarship? What if the competitive seasons overlap?

In addition, the student should ask herself all those questions everyone college-bound asks concerning location (distance from home, nearness to a city, climate), sex division (single-sex or coed, proportion of males to females), and size of the student body.

When the student finally gets down to applying for a scholarship, she should follow these tips:
  1. Type, do not write.
  2. Address letters to the Women's Athletic Director.
  3. Include personal information (name, address, height, weight) and relevant statistics (major accomplishments, times or scores, years of experience). Include nonscholastic competition.

A glowing letter from a high school or private coach might also prove helpful. The next step is to cross fingers and hope. Maybe the phone will start ringing and the mailbox will fill with offers from college recruiters.

There are strict rules regarding recruiting practices. These rules seem to change yearly, but the philosophy remains constant: keep commercialism and exploitation out of women's athletics. The goal is to avoid the high-pressure, wheeling-dealing tactics that often invade men's athletics, yet to give women opportunity for financial aid.

The AIAW has governed competition for women on the

local, state, regional, and national levels between colleges since 1971. However, in 1980, the male-oriented National Collegiate Athletic Association (NCAA) began vying for that privilege. The first NCAA women's championships are planned for the 1981–82 season. The power struggle between AIAW and NCAA to decide who will run women's sports promises to be vigorous. Rules may change as a result in both competition and recruiting policies.

The AIAW currently dictates recruitment policies. In its free *High School Brochure,* it spells out the rules for eligibility, financial aid, auditions, and letters of intent. This informative pamphlet is available through coaches and physical education teachers or by writing to the address listed at the back of the book.

Recruiters may contact a student athlete or her parents and coaches through letters and telephone calls, but not through private meetings at home or high school. They may, however, hold auditions on the college campus, for which the student pays her own expenses.

Interested colleges send a "letter of intent" on March 1, spelling out their offerings. The student must select one, and only one, within fourteen days.

Recruiters vying with one another, showering letters of intent and scholarship offers by the dozen—a college education —is it all an impossible dream? No.

The tickets to that dream are a reality. Jeannie Gilbert and Debbie Lytle have won theirs. Tickets are waiting for 9,998 more.

6. Helping Others

"Winning Is Everything" seems to be the motto of many athletes. But not all. Some believe that athletic talents are like a batch of warm brownies —they taste better when they're shared.

For example:

A high school softball pitcher volunteers to coach fourth-graders on a municipal team.

A ranked tennis player takes time off from her tournament circuit to conduct a free clinic for beginners.

An accomplished skier forsakes the challenge of conquering the experts' slopes for the challenge of teaching one special person on the beginners' slope.

Skiing brings to mind blue skies and sunshine, with vigorous happy people gliding over fluffy snow.

But at Lake Eldora, a small ski area in the foothills of Colorado's Rocky Mountains, stars and floodlights illuminate the well-groomed slopes. Some of the skiers are cold, clumsy, and crying with fright. Others are laughing with delight, even when they fall in a snowy heap.

Some are blind; some are retarded; some are amputees. But on Monday nights they learn to ski.

One of their instructors is Missy Myers, eighteen, a freshman at the University of Colorado at nearby Boulder. Dressed in a bright-orange parka and faded jeans, Missy relaxes by the fire in the wood-paneled lodge. She has just finished giving a ski lesson to Linda, a retarded eight-year-old from a special Denver school.

"Linda smiled at me today," Missy says. "This was a much better lesson than the first one, because now she knows my name and the feel of my arms. She knows I won't let her get hurt. I have to get her confidence one hundred percent or we can't do anything."

During the first lesson she remembers that Linda constantly said she needed to go to the bathroom. "We would just get started and she'd say she needed to go. So we'd take off our skis, struggle with her clothes, bundle her up, then go back outside, put on the skis, climb up the slope—and she'd need to go again.

"I was beginning to lose my patience," she recalls, "until I finally realized she was just plain scared. Skiing was strange to her and I was strange to her."

How did Missy gain Linda's confidence? By continuously talking to her in simple terms, explaining the equipment and gliding movements, and encouraging her as they sidestepped slowly up the gentle hill.

For the first trip down, Missy put her own skis in a snow-plow wedge on the outside of Linda's, while holding her firmly around the waist. Gradually the little girl's trembling subsided as they skied slowly down the hill together. She even wanted to try it again!

Later, they linked ski poles together and Missy snowplowed close behind Linda, talking all the while: "Go right, up weight, down weight." Linda was doing the legwork herself, yet had the security of being "attached" to her instructor through her ski poles.

Blind students are taught with similar methods, although the instructor may add directions from the clock face, such as "Mogul at 10 o'clock, turn left."

But the pupil's short attention span was a problem. "If her mind is somewhere else, forget it," Missy soon learned. "So you have to do something to get it back." She would pick Linda

Volunteer "Special Needs" instructors are rewarded by
the smiles of their students
Courtesy of Eldora Handicapped Recreation Program

up in her arms and give her a fast ride. Soon the little girl would
be clamoring to ski herself.

Both were encouraged. Linda was learning something about
skiing and Missy was learning something about disabled people.

"I had never even talked to a retarded person before," Missy
explains. "And I had never done volunteer work." But a college
poster recruiting instructors for a "special needs" skiing program attracted her attention. She was interested in teaching
sports and knew about the current push to help the disabled.
She attended six training sessions before being assigned a pupil
for five lessons.

After just two lessons with Linda, she has a number of new
convictions. "Many retarded people are teachable, especially
on a one-to-one basis," she feels. "They respond to someone

caring." And Missy wishes that everyone who teaches, whether school, music, or sports, could have the opportunity to work with the disabled, to understand their worlds as well as to appreciate able-bodied students better.

Missy herself began skiing in her sloping backyard when she was five. Along with her brother and sister, she was taught by her parents, much as she is teaching today.

"Later, I remember falling off rope tows and dangling from T bars." She ruffles her fingers through her short, curly red hair and laughs. "I remember flying down a hill in a snowplow, unable to turn, slow down, or stop any way but by falling down."

But formal instruction came with family ski weeks in Vermont. In the daily two-hour lessons, she mastered the snowplow, stem christies, and finally parallel skiing.

Often her friends, especially the better skiers, spurred her on to greater speed and daredevil stunts. "You can't cry or quit when you get cold or fall down if your friends are watching," she says. "You have to keep up and you learn fast!"

Does she like to compete in official races?

"Now I don't feel the urge to compete in skiing," she says. "I like to go where I want to go and stop when I want to stop and look at the views. I like skiing because it is peaceful and individual. And besides," she adds, "I get enough competition in tennis."

From the ages of ten to sixteen, Missy competed in scores of U.S. Tennis Association sanctioned tournaments. She played on high school and club teams and now is a member of the University of Colorado women's varsity tennis team.

At one point, her father asked her if she wanted to concentrate exclusively on tennis and try for the big leagues. But Missy also liked softball, basketball, and skiing, as well as Sunday afternoon touch football and even Ultimate Frisbee. She was unwilling to make a complete commitment to one sport.

"Different sports suit me for different reasons," she explains. "Team play, individuality, competition, or just plain fun."

The "killer instinct" she developed in tennis carries over into

Able-bodied Nancy Kalinski *(right)* helps an amputee master outrigger skis
Courtesy of Eldora Handicapped Recreation Program

other areas, she admits. "I have to curb my competitiveness so I don't try to outdo other people all the time or walk over them to make myself feel good.

"Teaching sports to other people is good for me," she adds. "I am learning to be patient, to encourage others, and to put myself in their shoes."

What does the future hold? She hopes her study of business and recreational management will eventually lead to a career in a resort area, a private club, or a public recreation department. But sometime before that, she wants to be a "ski bum."

The life of a ski bum in New England or the West used to be very glamorous and exciting—free room, free meals, free ski pass, and even a little extra "beer money." All that for just a few hours a day waiting tables or washing dishes. But those days may be gone forever, for today, ski bumming simply does not pay.

Most ski areas pay minimum wages, period. Unless they are bankrolled by their own savings or very generous parents, few young people can afford the expenses of lodging, meals, and lift tickets on the wages of a waitress or dishwasher.

Becoming a ski instructor is one possible answer. But how does one do that?

According to the Professional Ski Instructors of America (PSIA), "The best way to become an instructor is first to improve your skiing so that you are able to demonstrate all finished forms, such as snowplows, stem turns, stem christies, flawlessly. The best place to learn all this is in a recognized ski school.

"Study and read everything you can about skiing and ski techniques. And last, go to your local ski school director and tell him that you are interested in becoming a ski instructor and would like to work toward that goal. Ski school directors are always looking for people who qualify to work into apprentice capacities."

In preparation for certification, many courses are given throughout the United States, usually through individual ski schools. Costs vary according to geographical and individual areas, but are generally low.

The certification test is very thorough and the applicant must be recommended by her local ski school director before applying. A list of instructor divisions, where exams are given, is available from PSIA.

What are the benefits?

1. The personal satisfaction of becoming a proficient skier
2. The satisfaction of teaching skills to others and observing them become proficient
3. Meeting people with many different personalities and backgrounds
4. Recreational enjoyment of a dynamic and exciting sport
5. Vigorous and healthy occupation

6. Free use of ski lifts
7. Purchase of ski equipment from manufacturers at
   substantial discount

The pay for a ski instructor varies with geographical location and depends on whether she gives group or private lessons. Instructing may be part-time or full-time, but will never extend more than seven or eight hours a day.

Another way to get free skiing, as well as the satisfaction that comes from helping others, is to become a ski patroller. Dressed in the familiar rust-colored parka with a yellow cross on the back, a ski patroller gives first aid to victims of on-the-hill accidents as well as heart attacks. She may also take part in search and rescue, lift evacuation, and accident prevention programs.

Most members of the National Ski Patrol System are volunteers. But some full-time patrollers (sixteen or more hours per week) attain professional (paid) status.

Mary Bozack of Moretown, Vermont, is one of the few female certified professional patrollers in the system. Mary believes that today women patrollers are working extra hard to prove their capabilities. They want to avoid being treated as "second-rate patrollers," the ones who make coffee and clean the first-aid rooms. They replace physical strength with knowledge of fine sled-handling techniques.

Since the formation of the National Ski Patrol System in 1938, the requirements have been the same for women as for men. Although women are usually not expected to haul heavy equipment bags and toboggans back up on the surface lifts, they do run loaded sleds, give first aid, and ski all the trails.

The best women patrollers often become the training officers in their patrols. They are moving up through the ranks to hold leadership positions at patrol, section, region, division, and even national levels.

Naturally, extensive training is required to qualify as a ski patroller. According to the *Ski Patroller's Manual,* "A candidate must be at least eighteen years old, must hold a current American National Red Cross (ANRC) First Aid and Emergency Care or Emergency Medical Technician (EMT) certification, and must have sufficient skiing and toboggan handling ability to pass the NSPS Basic Ski Patrol Test."

At fifteen, one can register as a candidate for Junior Ski Patroller. As an apprentice, she learns the disciplines and dedication of ski patrolling, while putting into practice the skills acquired during candidate training.

At eighteen, she automatically becomes a full-fledged Ski Patroller. Those interested in the program should contact the Ski Patrol Leader at the nearest ski area.

As the manual points out, "The Junior Ski Patrol is an area in society in which young people can exercise their inherent desires to do something worthwhile—to help their fellow men and to gain the respect of their peers and elders."

Skiing can be more than "catching the rays" under sunny skies, speeding over powdery snow and enjoying breathtaking views.

It can be helping, teaching, and guiding others. In skiing, as in other sports, sharing one's athletic ability can bring the inner glow of satisfaction that Missy feels when she says, "Linda smiled at me today."

7. Exploding Old Myths

Once upon a time, not so very long ago, the most active sport for girls was lawn croquet at summer picnics. Everybody believed that girls were too delicate for athletics. Strenuous exercise could even be harmful to girls, the old myths said.

In recent years, scientists, coaches, athletic trainers, and sports-loving girls have been working hard to explode the old myths. Small-group studies and individual experience have provided more realistic views.

Fortunately attitudes are changing. Today's girls are allowed onto the playing fields and courts and tracks all over the world. They can wear shorts instead of long skirts, T-shirts instead of middy blouses.

So are the old myths dead? No. Because old myths die hard. Even when they are disproved by factual evidence, they lurk under the surface.

The best way to explode the myths about girls and sports is to expose them to the light of day. Then one must examine them in view of current research and personal experience.

The myths revolve around three basic themes:

Girls are too delicate for sports.

Female reproductive systems are harmed by vigorous activity.

Masculine traits appear in female athletes.

Whatever happened to the delicate lawn croquet players
of yesteryear?

Are girls really more delicate than boys? Are they injured
more easily or more often while playing sports? "No," says Dr.
Dorothy Harris, who is head of the Center for Women and
Sport at Pennsylvania State University. "It's safe to say there
is no significant difference in injury statistics between men and
women athletes when proper conditioning, training, and medi-

cal services are available to both."

Dr. Harris' research has shown that one's level of physical fitness is more significant than sex in determining the effects of exercise.

In fact, girls have the capability to equal or even outperform boys in athletic feats from the ages of ten to fourteen. Girls' earlier growth spurt gives them an advantage during these years.

Marge Albohm, head women's athletic trainer at Indiana University, explains that females begin their adolescent growth spurt between ten and a half and thirteen years. This ends at the onset of menstruation and total growth ends at about sixteen. Boys, meanwhile, do not begin their growth spurt until twelve and a half to fifteen years.

Evidence of equal work capacity between boys and girls aged ten to fourteen led to the revolutionary admitting of girls to Little League Baseball in 1972 (see Chapter 12). But most authorities join Ms. Albohm in disapproving of mixed athletic competition in contact sports because, after puberty (about fifteen), males become considerably stronger, taller, and heavier than girls. They have greater muscular and cardiovascular endurance and excel in most motor skills.

Of course, one difference between boys and girls is that girls have breasts. Part of the delicacy myth is that girls' breasts make them vulnerable. "Breasts are less susceptible to injury than knees or elbows, whether male or female," says P. S. Wood in a *New York Times Magazine* article on sex difference in sports. And he adds that the suspicion that severe bruises cause breast cancer is simply not borne out by research.

Breasts can be a problem for some girls in sports, however. Many full-busted girls (with a C or D cup bra) have shied away from sports because bouncing was painful or because they felt thrown off balance. Smaller-busted girls who exercised braless sometimes experienced sagging due to gradual collagen tissue breakdown.

At long last, someone has recognized the problem and done something about it. Two enterprising women invented the first sports bra by sewing two jockstraps together!

An authority on sports-related injuries to women, Dr. Christine Haycock of the New Jersey School of Medicine, took a plastic female torso and a selection of sports bras on television talk shows last year. She stressed the importance of firm support and comfort for females who exercise vigorously.

"Choose a bra that limits up-and-down motion," Dr. Haycock advised. "It should be absorbent and allow air circulation. It should be nonabrasive, with no hardware to dig into the flesh. The bra should not ride up in front and straps should not fall off the shoulders." She adds that there is no tissue damage or sagging when breasts are properly supported.

Now for the subject of menstruation. Some people believe that women do not function at peak performance during the menstrual period. They have sometimes used this argument in business as well as sports to prevent females from advancing.

Naturally, menstrual discomfort varies with the individual. Some girls do experience cramps, bloating, or irritability during periods. But many girls feel that exercising, rather than being harmful during a period, can actually relieve cramps and back pain. "I feel better if I do run than if I don't," claims one girl.

"There is even considerable evidence that athletic performance does not vary with the phases of the menstrual cycle," writes Elaine Pinkerton in a *Runner's World* article. A survey taken during the 1964 and 1968 Olympics showed that women set records in many events before, during, and after menstruation.

Irregular menstruation has become rather common among females involved in endurance exercises, such as long-distance running and swimming. Even ballet dancers, gymnasts, and tennis players may experience irregularity of periods.

For example, one freshman returned home after a rigorous year of training on a college tennis team. She reported that she had not had any periods during the entire school term, yet they started again when she came home. The gynecologist examining her said, "Oh, you were probably just homesick." Perhaps he was correct, or perhaps he should have investigated her activities more thoroughly.

Some doctors know so little about this subject that they fail to link strenuous exercise with menstrual irregularities. New research is now being conducted.

It appears that perhaps one out of five female athletes undergoing strenuous training experiences complete stopping of menstruation or secondary amenorrhea at some point. According to Thomas D. Fahey, this phenomenon seems to be related to a critical level of body fat. "Women who drop below sixteen percent fat seem to have irregular menstrual periods," he notes. Twenty percent fat level is standard in women.

Some women have secondary amenorrhea with an increase in training, then later resume their cycles and return to their original fat levels. This happened with the freshman tennis player.

Some authorities hold differing views. Dr. John Marshall, cochairman of the New York Medical Society's Committee on the Medical Aspects of Sports, believes that body fat percentage is not the only factor causing secondary amenorrhea. He recently reported, "All kinds of things we don't know about the delicate balance of hormones have an effect on it. It may have to do with the kind of training, or it may be psychological." He advises that a physician be consulted about the problem.

Young female endurance athletes sometimes have late menarche (first menstruation). For instance, one "toothpick" gymnast, who had trained and competed since she was seven, had never had a period by the time she was seventeen. A specialist advised her to ease away from competition for a while.

Does all this mean a female athlete may not be able to have babies? Tennis player Evonne Goolagong Cawley, swimmer Wendy Bogliolie, track star Wilma Rudolph, and gymnast Olga Korbut would certainly respond with a hearty laugh. They number among thousands of fine athletes who have become pregnant after many years of training for their sport.

The female reproductive organs are internal and well protected from shock. The uterus is much like an egg floating in a vacuum-sealed jar filled to the brim with water. Unless the jar is shattered, the egg will withstand any movement without breaking.

Doctors today frequently advise their patients to continue their athletic schedules well into pregnancy. Furthermore, researchers have found no evidence to show that physical activity hinders actual child-bearing. In one group study labor was actually found to be shorter among athletes than nonathletes.

What about masculine traits? Some girls fear they will develop bulging muscles through athletics. The experts agree that the development of bulging muscles depends mostly on the amount of male hormone (testosterone) a person has, not the amount of exercise. All people have some male hormones and some female hormones (estrogen). The balance of hormones determines many traits; exercise does not.

A few win-at-any-cost female athletes have taken anabolic steroids to improve their performance. These medications are extremely dangerous and should be avoided. Among the side effects are disruption of normal growth patterns, voice changes, acne, and hairiness.

"The long-term effects on reproductive function are not known now, but anabolic steroids may be harmful in this area," reports an article in *The Physician and Sportsmedicine.* And their ability to interfere with the menstrual cycle is well documented.

For these reasons, all concerned with advising, training, coaching, and providing medical care for female athletes should prevent their use of anabolic steroids.

Girls are sometimes embarrassed to discuss intimate questions with parents, doctors, or even coaches. This is one reason why so much mistaken belief surrounds the field of girls and sports.

Perhaps girls can have frank discussions with an expert on physical fitness—an athletic trainer. No, the athletic trainer does not train athletes in skills; the coach does that. The athletic trainer's job is to get and keep the athlete's body in good condition. He or she aims to prevent injuries, to provide first-aid treatment, and to rehabilitate the athlete after injury.

In college, the athletic trainer has studied anatomy; psychology; physiology of exercise; kinesiology; first aid and CPR (cardiopulmonary resuscitation); nutrition; personal, community, and school health; remedial exercise; and techniques of athletic training.

She has also logged six hundred hours of clinical experience over a two-year period, as required by the National Trainers Association. Before she becomes certified, she must earn a college degree with a teaching certificate.

Athletic training is an exciting new career possibility for women. Today, high schools, colleges, and professional teams are realizing the importance of having an athletic trainer on their sports staff. As girls' participation in sports increases, the number of positions for female athletic trainers should increase as well.

Karen Dove and Roberta Butler are two young women who hold challenging jobs in this field. Although their geographical locations and working conditions differ greatly, they share many of the same opinions regarding the girls' sports myths.

Karen benefited from the progressive attitude about the need for athletic trainers in the State of Texas. In her district, north of Houston, each high school is required to hire one male and one female athletic trainer.

"They came looking for me," Karen recalls happily. "They needed a female trainer for Conroe High School, so they offered me the job!"

Karen's performance on written exams had attracted the administration's attention. After receiving her master's degree in physical education at Sam Houston State (Huntsville), she had passed the state licensing test and national certification examination. She also held the necessary teaching certificate.

When Karen entered college six years ago, she didn't even know what an athletic trainer was. "My high school in Van, Texas, was so small that the only sport offered for girls was volleyball," she remembers. "They certainly didn't have a girls' athletic trainer."

So Karen played on the college varsity volleyball team. She

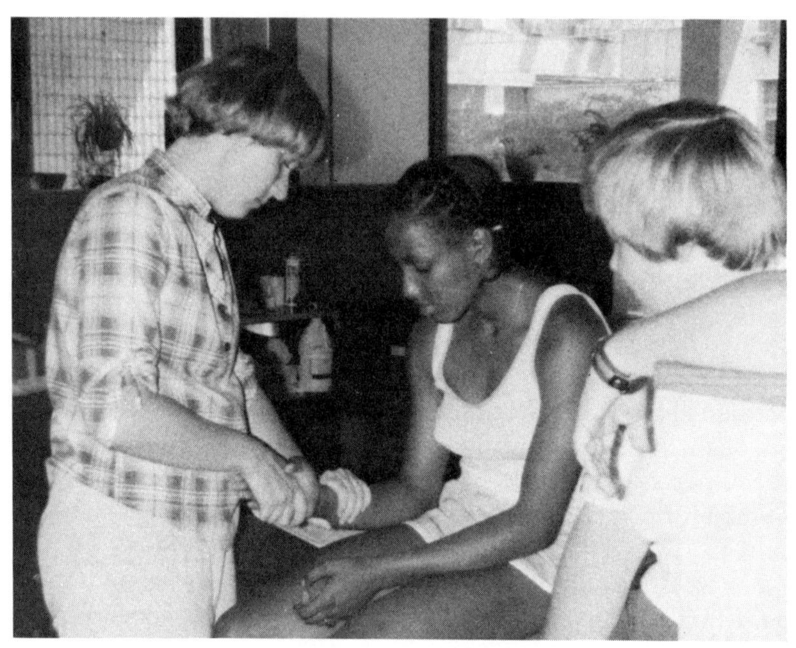

Athletic trainer Roberta Butler prescribes rehabilitation therapy for injured athletes

Gail Andersen Myers

expected to major in physical education with an emphasis on coaching. But after two years her direction changed. "I stopped playing on the team and became the manager," she says. "I became more and more interested in first aid and conditioning. Because of Title IX legislation and more opportunities for women in sports, I decided on a career as an athletic trainer." She teaches physical education and health classes in addition to her duties as trainer.

Roberta Butler also benefited from the increasing interest in sports medicine. She is an athletic trainer in the Temple University Center for Sports Medicine and Science in Philadelphia. In 1975, this became the first sports medicine center affiliated with a medical school.

Similar centers are springing up across the country. No

longer must an injured athlete search desperately for a sympathetic "jock doc."

The staff of the center includes orthopedic surgeons, cardiologists, and physical therapists as well as athletic trainers. In addition to injured high school, college, and pro athletes, they treat retired golfers with backaches as well as housewives with gardener's elbow. Whirlpools, exercise machines, massage, and taping are available to patients who pay a fee for the services.

Prevention of injury is one of the main goals of an athletic trainer. Roberta assists in runners' clinics and physical fitness programs as part of her job at the center. "As people learn to condition their bodies better they will have fewer injuries," she believes.

Roberta can sympathize with injured athletes. She suffered tendonitis and foot and knee injuries during her years of play-

Like their male counterparts, many female athletes now take part in year-round conditioning, weight lifting, and physical fitness programs
Carol Martin, Abington, Pa., YMCA

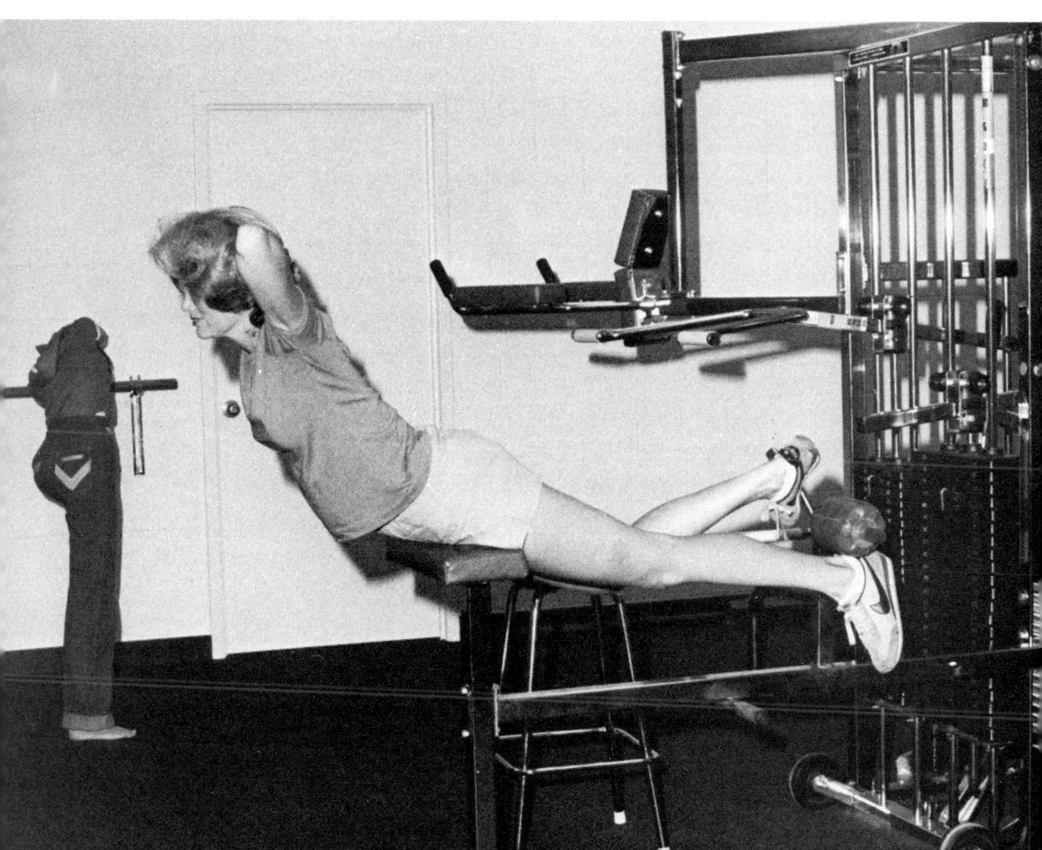

ing field hockey, lacrosse, and basketball at Abington High School.

"I can understand their desire to get back into action," she says. "We try to make sure they get back safely as well as quickly."

Roberta and Karen were not hired to treat females only. They also treat males for all kinds of injuries. Does this cause any problems?

"No problem," answers Karen in her soft Southwestern drawl. "The boys are respectful. They accept me strictly as a trainer—no differently from if I were a male."

Roberta agrees. But her blue eyes twinkle as she recalls one incident early in her career. A football player came in with a pulled groin muscle.

"I told him to drop his pants. He sure looked startled and so did the other boys in the training room at the time. But they soon got used to the idea that I'm no different from a nurse or a doctor or a coach. I'm strictly an athletic trainer!"

Both young women have had many opportunities to talk with female athletes about their physical problems. Roberta has noticed that intensive training and distance sports often stop menstruation. But cycles resume after training stops. For girls whose periods continue, exercise usually lessens severe cramps or premenstrual tension.

Karen notes that athletes seldom complain about their periods. "Oh, some do in gym classes or in junior high, but by the time they reach high school, they accept it as part of life."

The sports-related injuries of girls seem less serious than those of boys in the 3,500-student high school where Karen works. They are usually simple knee, back, or ankle sprains, whereas the boys have more broken bones or injuries requiring surgery. However, Karen sees that the number of girls participating is increasing. And girls are becoming more competitive and aggressive in sports.

"Possibly the number and severity of injuries will increase," she predicts. "On the other hand, girls are better coached now than in years past. And they are in much better physical condition."

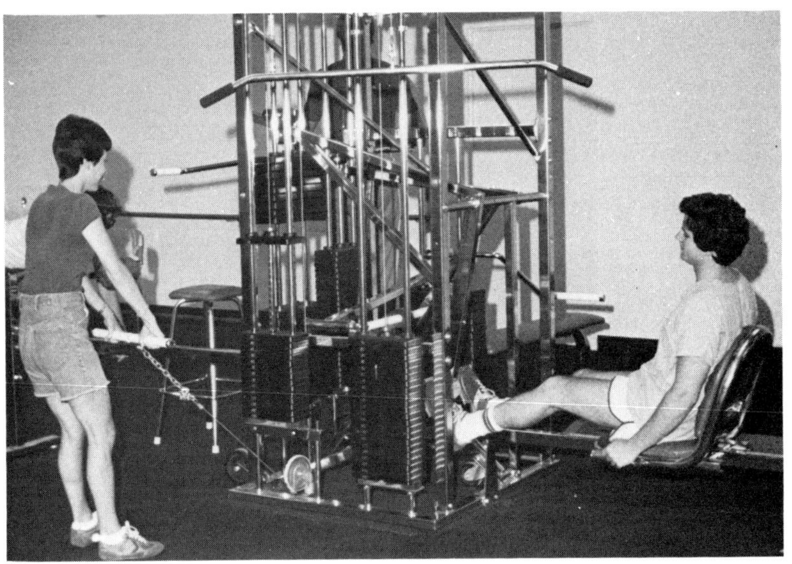

The physical fitness boom has brought thousands of people to fitness centers, such as this one at the Abington, Pa., YMCA, which features Universal Gym equipment
Carol Martin, Abington, Pa., YMCA

For today's female athletes, being in "good shape" means more than just looking great in a bikini. They want to be in top physical condition. Just like their male counterparts, many take part in year-round conditioning, weight lifting, and physical fitness programs.

Changing attitudes have made it okay for females to be competitive, aggressive, and hardworking. They can even sweat.

Where is the delicate croquet player of yesteryear? She might even have trouble recognizing herself as the panting, shorts-clad marathon runner of today. She has come a long way.

She is capable of going a lot farther. Exploding old myths is a crucial step.

8. Benefiting from New Laws

Which came first, new attitudes or new laws? Pondering that question from a spot in the middle of the action is the physical education teacher. Even she seems new.

In some people's minds, gym teachers used to be stereotyped as crusty drill sergeants who blew whistles and barked orders.

Karen Burrell Orr is one of many gym teachers who shatter that stereotype—she is young, petite, married. And coaching a lacrosse game on a May afternoon, she sounds more like a cheerleader than a Marine.

"Hurry up, Colleen, catch your girl!" she calls to one of the twenty-four short-skirted players racing toward a wire goal on the unboundaried field. "Check her, check her!"

But the opposing wing bobs and weaves through the home team, flips the ball past the goalie, and makes the score 8–7. Coach Orr bangs her hand on her forehead, tugs at her short brown hair.

Then one of her gold-jerseyed players catches the ball deftly in the net of her crosse. "Cradle, Monica, cradle!" shouts the pacing coach. So Monica keeps possession of the ball by twisting the stick with two hands while running downfield. Approaching the goal, she passes to a redheaded teammate, who catches it and flicks it into the goal to score the tying point.

"Good job, Ellen!" yells the coach, flinging both arms in the air.

Today, at twenty-seven, Karen Orr is just as enthusiastic about sports as she was ten years ago, when she was a star athlete at Upper Moreland High School, the very same school where she now teaches physical education and health classes. She also coaches a sport every season—field hockey, basketball, and lacrosse.

Unwinding in the faculty room after the game, she is cool and trim in a delicately striped blouse, bright-red kilt, and sneakers. As she gestures while talking, the rings glittering on her left hand indicate her new status—a married woman for less than a month.

"You would be amazed at the difference the rings and a marriage license make," she confides. "The change in attitude is very subtle, but now I feel more respect from my students, their parents, the administration, and other teachers. Suddenly I've come of age, I'm legitimate, I'm stable. And yet," she adds with a smile, "I know I'm the same person I was a month ago."

Karen is very conscious of the attitudes, stereotypes, and stigmas surrounding not only physical education teachers but all female athletes as well.

Although attitudes are changing, she feels it is only now becoming acceptable for a girl to be dedicated to sports. Until now, a female has had to pretend to be not very interested or else she has had to go it alone. But if she has chosen to spend a great deal of time and effort on her sports in the company of other females, she has run the risk of being called "gay."

"Gay" is a term widely used and abused today, even in elementary schools, to mean homosexual. A homosexual is a person who prefers a male-male or female-female sexual relationship. A "straight" in current slang is a person who prefers a male-female relationship.

"Face it," Karen says bluntly. "There *are* gays in women's sports—in softball, tennis, field hockey, all of them. Not so much on the high school level, but on the college and professional level. Maybe the stereotyping made them that way. But there are plenty of straights, too. They can coexist. The problems come when girls are not aware of the differences."

Growing up in a family of three boys and three girls, Karen

Karen Burell Orr, shown on baseball and hockey fields,
coaches a varsity sport every season

Gail Andersen Myers

felt it was perfectly okay to play sports wholeheartedly. From
seventh grade on, she played field hockey and basketball, adding softball and track in high school. Because she was a star
athlete, everyone expected her to become a physical education
teacher. She had few other choices; she fell into that track as
a matter of course.

She remembers that when she went off to college, one that
specialized in physical education, she was too naive to know
anything about homosexuality. Therefore, she was shocked to
find that the athletic teams were divided into "camps" of
straights and gays, with each group trying to win the other
over to its thinking and sororities.

Once, when a team was divided four to one, and she was the
one straight, she began to question herself: They love sports
and I love sports—so what am I?

In experiences such as this every girl may be assailed by
confusion and self-doubt, unless she is aware that differences
in people do exist. She learns to hold on to her own values. She
needs to realize that some "friendly" gestures have meanings
undesirable for her.

"Awareness is the key," believes Karen, who instructs coed

classes in human sexuality and health with the intention of airing these and other problems openly.

While she holds no prejudice against men coaching girls' teams, she finds that girls feel more comfortable discussing personal problems or ailments, particularly those related to menstrual periods, with a female coach. Nevertheless, more than once she has told a girl complaining of cramps, "Okay, I understand. Now get out there and play!"

Her own experience has led her to take a very serious view of physical injuries, however. As a senior in high school, she suffered a knee injury. A crucial basketball game was scheduled before she fully recovered. But because she was the leading scorer, the coach insisted she play.

"Ten years later, I still resent that," she declares. "Nobody wants to win more than I do, but there is a limit to what you can ask of a player. I will never send a person into a game if she is not physically fit, no matter how crucial the game."

In addition to teaching and coaching, promoting awareness of athletic opportunities is also the job of a physical education teacher. Karen is particularly excited about the opportunities for women in field hockey, which in 1980 was included for the first time in the Olympics.

She herself had hoped to make the United States team. Very recently she trained rigorously for two years and attended a developmental camp conducted by the United States Field Hockey Association (USFHA) at Penn State. But after progressing from C level to B level, she was eliminated because she was too old.

"Today they are looking for seventeen- and eighteen-year-olds, and even younger, to mold a team for the 1984 Olympics. I just wish they had told me earlier I was 'over the hill,'" she says a bit ruefully. So even a coach can get cut from the team!

As a coach, however, she realizes the importance of selecting promising younger players. "I will often work with freshmen and sophomores more than with seniors and give them opportunities to play," she says. "We can develop their skills and bring them along for the future. As in most sports, the earlier they start, the better their chances."

Not all girls are team caliber, though. People often ask Karen if she becomes frustrated or bored teaching uncoordinated or clumsy students in required gym classes.

"No," she answers, "because I understand their limitations and I like the challenge of working with them. It's the talented athletes—the ones with real potential—who sometimes frustrate me, when they won't discipline themselves, practice, or work to their potential. I demand a lot from them."

While some players become emotional or resentful over her methods, most realize her wisdom. As one veteran team player put it: "She's tough. But nobody ever complains about what she teaches you!"

Karen advises students interested in field hockey to obtain information from the USFHA about the regional developmental programs. College teams compete in the AIAW-sponsored tournaments, but noncollege players may join local field hockey clubs and sectional associations.

Several other sports are rapidly gaining popularity in girls' athletic programs. High schools are currently adding lacrosse, track, volleyball, soccer, and softball as interest develops.

Why? Because Title IX says they must. Title IX, which is a section of the Education Amendments Act passed by Congress in 1972, has changed the course of women's sports forever. History may even rank it alongside the Nineteenth Amendment, allowing women the right to vote in 1920, or the controversial Equal Rights Amendment of the 1970's and '80s.

Title IX states in part:

> No person in the United States shall, on the basis of sex, be excluded from participation in, be denied the benefits of, or be subjected to discrimination under any education program or activity receiving federal financial assistance.

This law was intended to give girls opportunities equal to those of boys in all areas of education, not just sports. But it is not so simple as it seems, for equality works both ways.

Many people predicted that the legislation would backfire, and they were right. Almost the next day, five burly football players at a New England high school showed up for girls'

Because of Title IX, women can play many more high school sports

Charles Gilbert

softball tryouts. They loudly proclaimed that they were being discriminated against if they could not join the team. The local authorities dismissed it as the prank it was meant to be and said, in essence: "Forget it, fellas!"

Others would not "forget it," however. And the 1975 attempt by the federal Department of Health, Education, and Welfare (HEW) to spell out guidelines for "equal opportunity for members of both sexes," particularly in noncontact sports, gave rise to some bizarre interpretations and testings of the law.

For example, in May 1979, a U.S. District Court judge in Providence, Rhode Island, ruled that a six-foot tall male high school senior was unconstitutionally barred from the girls' volleyball team and ordered that he be allowed to play. The Rhode Island Interscholastic League planned to appeal the ruling, however, believing it could mean that "a lot of boys who can't make the boys' teams will try out for the girls' teams." Many people fear that rulings of this sort could ruin girls' sports programs.

Yet, just two weeks later, the Supreme Court handed down a ruling on quite a different case, which was hailed by women's rights leaders as an important victory. In *Cannon* v. *University of Chicago,* a thirty-nine-year-old nurse claimed that sex discrimination was the reason she was denied admission to medical school.

She was suing the University of Chicago and Northwestern University for not adhering to Title IX. By granting Nurse Cannon's suit, the Supreme Court gave individuals, not just the government, the right to bring sex-discrimination suits against federally funded schools and colleges.

Maybe not too many athletes would ask for the trouble and expense of going to court in order to play on a volleyball or soccer team. What else can they do?

If they feel discriminated against, they can complain to the Department of Health and Human Services, which now sets the guidelines for carrying out Title IX and pays attention to public reaction to all Title IX policy. A letter should be directed to: Director, Office for Civil Rights, U.S. Department of Education, Washington, DC 20201. Regional offices of the Office for Civil Rights may also be contacted. An investigator will be sent to the individual school to look into the complaint.

A model letter for filing a complaint appears at the back of this book. It was prepared by the Women's Equity Action League Educational and Legal Defense Fund (WEAL Fund). This is a nonprofit, Washington-based organization that supports litigation (court cases), conducts research, and publishes information on sex discrimination.

"You have questions? SPRINT has answers!" proclaims SPRINT, a WEAL Fund project that serves as a national clearinghouse for information on sex discrimination in sports.

By telephoning the toll-free SPRINT-line (800) 424-5162, one can obtain straightforward answers to such questions as:

What are my rights?

Who must comply?

Who can help me?

How do I complain?

What else can I do?

Answering a SPRINT-line call, Char Millison, assistant director of the project, reported that most complaints deal with "across the board, broad-based discrimination." Specific complaints deal with the fewer sports offered for girls, lower level of competition, inadequate number of coaches and assistants, limited access to facilities or incomparable facilities, poor scheduling of games and practices, lower budgets for equipment.

On the college level, complaints also deal with travel money and per diem expenses as well as athletic scholarships.

Free of charge, SPRINT also provides contacts and referrals, technical assistance, political strategies, scholarship information, and, perhaps best of all, moral support. Its fast-paced newspaper, *In the Running,* reports the latest news and analyses of issues affecting girls and women in sports.

Are the efforts of individuals and groups really getting results?

"Definitely!" says Linda Cassady, a suburban high school coach. "In the last two years we have added girls' track, softball, and cross-country to our program. And we are getting more money for equipment and uniforms now." She recalls that three years ago, she ordered warm-up suits for the girls' tennis team. They arrived halfway through the season! And those suits had to be passed on to the basketball team and then to the lacrosse team.

"But this year," she adds, "one week before school started, the administration decided to field a girls' cross-country team. The uniforms arrived on the first day of school!"

The number of girls participating in athletics has dramatically increased since the enactment of Title IX. According to the National Federation of State High School Associations, only 317,000 girls took part in school sports in 1972. By 1978, 2,083,000 girls participated—a 550 percent increase. In the same period, the number of boys participating in sports increased only 16 percent.

Inequities still exist in school sports programs. Salaries for coaches and officials of girls' sports are often lower than those for boys' sports. The National Association for Girls and Women in Sport (NAGWS) is one agency working to eliminate inequities in hiring, promotion, and pay. The Equal Employment Opportunity Commission (EEOC) is another.

The women's liberation movement has done much to help the cause of women in sports. Many believe that passage of the Equal Rights Amendment (ERA) will produce many more opportunities for women in all areas. Section 1 of the proposed amendment states:

> Equality of rights under the law shall not be denied or abridged by the United States or any state on account of sex.

If the ERA becomes part of the U.S. Constitution, new laws will undoubtedly be written that will affect female athletes.

The question "Which came first, new attitudes or new laws?" may never be answered. Perhaps it doesn't matter. What does matter is that, as Karen Burrell Orr puts it, "Today a girl can be accepted for what she is. And she doesn't have to go it alone anymore."

9. Coaching and Teaching

In the past, a female athlete had to make difficult choices, combine different options:

Shall I choose coaching or a playing career?

Shall I choose coaching or marriage?

Shall I choose coaching or raising a family?

Today she can successfuly intertwine a coaching or teaching career with her changing life-styles as a playing professional, a single, a wife, or a mother.

The main attraction of coaching is flexibility. A woman may devote as much or as little time to it as she herself chooses. She can often select her own hours, places, and pupils.

Her financial rewards vary according to her own ambition, ability, and ingenuity.

Coaching and teaching opportunities exist for women today as never before in history. Here's why:

Since Title IX passed, girls are participating in sports in record numbers—they need coaches.

Due to the physical fitness boom, people of all ages are learning lifetime sports—they seek instructors.

Because of increasing monetary rewards, many athletes strive to excel—they want expert coaches.

Barbara Maltby demonstrates the perfect form that makes
her number one female squash player

Karen Kelso

Smart women are carefully analyzing this tempting variety of opportunities. Some are hungrily grabbing opportunities that already exist. Others are inventing unusual combinations of their own.

The true stories of three female coach/teachers illustrate some of the many ways a woman can have a successful coaching career and her choice of life-style as well.

Barbara Maltby, for example, combines coaching with a professional playing career. As the number one female squash player in the United States, she now has pupils standing in line to take lessons.

"Barbara is my idol," declares one enthusiastic pupil, seventeen-year-old Karen Kelso. "Her form is perfect. I feel so lucky to be working with her!" Karen, who is currently ranked No. 2 nationally in her age group, was a member of the U.S. girls' team that won the First ISRF World Junior Squash Championships held in Sweden in 1980. She attributes much of her success to Barbara's coaching.

Barbara demonstrates her teaching and playing skills at the Washington Square Racquets Club, which perches high above Philadelphia's traffic-clogged streets. Enclosed in a small (18½' $\times$ 32') white, red-lined squash court, she is in perpetual motion. She whirls, twirls, and leaps; she stretches, slashes, and lunges. She never takes her eye off the hard little black ball. Soon her exhausted pupil is wringing wet.

But Barbara emerges smiling and cool in trim yellow shorts and top. Her sleek brown pixie-style hairdo is barely ruffled.

At thirty-one, she has the look of a wide-eyed teenager. But inside that youthful and athletic figure is the mind of a clever and determined businesswoman. She studies the changing women's sports market and adjusts her goals accordingly.

At the University of Pennsylvania, Barbara played varsity softball, field hockey, and basketball. She loved sports and wanted to continue.

"But after graduation, I was at a dead end," she recalls. "There were no women's professional teams at that time. I couldn't find enough people to practice with. So I decided to switch to the lifetime sports."

She took up tennis and did well in local and regional tournaments. She even played in the European tennis circuit. But she soon realized that her chances of reaching the top were slim. "I would have had to move to some state where I could practice and play all year round—maybe Florida or California. I didn't want to do that."

She had competitive drive, energy, and athletic talent, but she didn't know where to put it. Then fate stepped in.

"I was working as a medical technician, doing pulmonary research on small animals," she relates. "One day a co-worker said he needed a partner to play squash on his lunch hour. He gave me a racquet and showed me how to play."

A year later, she was beating him. Then she began working with the Cynwyd Club's Norm Bramall, who had coached six national champions. He taught her finesse and basic strategies. Then he gave her a schedule of women's squash tournaments and encouraged her to enter.

Barbara scored victories and captured titles around the country. Like a small tornado, she whirled and twirled her way to the number one ranking in 1976. She held on to that top spot for four more years.

The one title that kept eluding her was the Women's Singles Championships. For four years she was a finalist, but never the winner. But 1980 was different—she won the tournament without losing a single game. *Squash News* reported that when the trophy was presented to her after the finals match, Barbara exclaimed, "I don't usually feel this way at this time of year —*great!*"

But the prize money and teaching fees were not enough to provide a living. She began looking for other sources of income. She found that exhibitions and clinics paid well. And endorsements from equipment, clothing, and sneaker manufacturers could be very lucrative. In return for the fees, she simply would use or wear the products in tournaments and exhibitions.

To make the most advantage of these possibilities, she hired an agent, the International Management Group of Cleveland.

"Because of her clients in many sports, an agent has contacts in the promotional departments of the sports companies," Barbara explains. "She can get you endorsements, speaking engagements, advertisements, and exhibitions."

Barbara believes strongly in promoting the entire sport of squash, not just herself. Right now she is working with several others to form the Association of Professional Women's Squash. They hope for more prize-money tournaments, perhaps even a Grand Prix Circuit, with bigger purses as well as television coverage.

"We need unity and we need to go as a group to sponsors and tournaments," she declares.

Barbara sees a big boom coming in squash. "It is an urban sport," she says. "It is played indoors almost all year round. You don't need big spaces to play and you don't need a lot of time—you can get a good workout in forty-five minutes. Business people like it because they can play during lunch hours or right after work."

Squash courts are popping up in cities around the country. New York City is booming with courts, as are East Coast cities from Boston to Washington, West Coast cities from Seattle to Los Angeles, and Chicago and Detroit in the middle.

"Every one of those clubs needs a professional," Barbara says. "The opportunities for women are there."

Her big hazel eyes take on a faraway look. "And then there's racquetball, too," she says. "I've been fooling around with that a little bit lately." One can only guess what her next step will be.

Far off in the rolling farmlands of Vermont, meanwhile, Suzie Merrill Grimes is recalling the steps she took that allowed her to choose a sports career and a life-style.

Suzie combines her job as swimming coordinator and instructor for the City of St. Albans with her role of wife and mother. She adds to the family income, and she has something concrete to show for her efforts—a large in-ground swimming pool perched on a tree-shaded ridge in her own backyard.

Dressed in her "working uniform," a bright red T-back

"Learning to swim should be fun," says Suzie Merrill Grimes. Her business is in her own backyard.

Chris Grimes

bathing suit, she waves a tanned hand at the sparkling pool. "It's incredibly good for my ego," she says. "Nobody gave me that. I got it myself."

It wasn't easy. She had three active preschool boys to raise, dogs and horses to tend, and a huge Victorian house to restore.

But Suzie has always had energy to burn. Even in her private school days, she used to ride horses between classes just to let off steam.

Later, as a young rural housewife, she wanted an occupation that would produce income but not interfere with her family life. She thoughtfully examined her training, skills, and experience. Her degree in hotel management might be helpful in organizing her active household, but it was not practical for a commercial venture right then.

Her sewing abilities led her to tailor clothes for others. "But I got frustrated, because people don't know what they want," she says. "They don't know what looks good on them."

Then she thought about her many summers swimming, boating, and water-skiing at Lake George, New York. She had taken lifesaving courses and had enjoyed teaching children at day camps. She had also recently worked as a volunteer in the city's swim program.

Suzie and her husband, Chris, had often dreamed of putting a swimming pool at the back of their property. But there were too many other bills to be paid. If only there were some way a pool could be a business venture.

She asked the Small Business Administration and the Internal Revenue Service for pamphlets and advice. "I always get my answers in writing," she says.

The Small Business Administration offers free counseling on loans, record-keeping, licenses, and other aspects of starting and managing a home business.

The Internal Revenue Service offers helpful pamphlets, such as Publication 587, *Business Use of Your Home.* Both agencies are listed under U.S. Government in local telephone directories.

Suzie also began updating her skills. She took courses for American Red Cross certification as senior lifesaver, WSI (Water Safety Instructor) and TI (Teacher Instructor).

"Then I heard about a part-time position as swimming coordinator. I applied for the job as if it were for the presidency of General Motors," she declares with her usual breathless enthusiasm. She gave her credentials, her experience, and her teaching philosophy, "I believe a regimented program is fruitful, but I also allow pupils to grow at their own speed. Learning to swim should be fun."

She convinced the recreation department that her age, maturity, and experience as a mother were plus factors. She got the job. Then she took out a loan and had the pool built.

Weekday mornings she worked in the municipal office coordinating, and afternoons she conducted private group lessons, lifesaving and WSI classes, in her own pool. She was also careful to allot time for playing with her own children in between.

Business problems quickly arose, however. She learned from

experience that she must keep accurate records and receipts of every expense if she wanted to cover expenses and make a profit. Water, electricity, chemicals, repairs, insurance, kickboards, and even a mother's helper for her children were all legitimate business expenses.

"Those nickels and dimes mount up—you have to keep track of them if you want to make a profit," she explains. "A small business can be lucrative if you know the law."

With careful planning, she will have her pool expenses covered, her loan paid off, and some extra income. So she has her swimming pool, her business, and her family, all in her own backyard. What more could she want?

"Well," she says with another wave of her tanned hand, "there's a spot over there that would be just right for a tennis court. I've been thinking."

Also doing some thinking in suburban Phoenixville, Pennsylvania, is Lucie McAvoy. Lucie was married, too, but her children were leaving the nest. She played and taught tennis during the warm months of the year, but she wanted some vigorous outdoor activity in the blustery cold winter months.

Having grown up in "the home of platform tennis," Scarsdale, New York, she was an accomplished paddle player. But the game hadn't yet caught on in the new area to which she had moved. The only way she could play was to enter regional tournaments. This meant traveling long distances.

One winter day, during a lengthy drive home from a tournament with her partner, Mig Simpson, she was bemoaning the fact that they had to go so far for a decent paddle game. Nobody around home knew how to play. So right then and there, she decided to teach a few people how.

She and Mig began by teaching groups of Waynesborough Country Club friends just for fun. But word spread quickly, and soon other Main Line clubs invited her to teach their members.

When she realized that she could turn fun into profit, Lucie formed a company called Paddle, Ltd. She added several women and a couple of men to the staff and began scheduling

"Stand your ground at the net—in the 'thrust' position," platform tennis instructor Lucie McAvoy advises Nan Hamilton *(right)* and Sue Sayer *(left)*

Times–Chronicle

clinics at clubs around the area and in neighboring states.

Women's clinics for groups of four were usually four weekly one-and-a-half-hour sessions, with a minimum of sixteen participants and two instructors. Men's clinics usually ran just one session for groups of four with one instructor.

Expenses were low. The clubs provided their own courts, so Lucie didn't even have to rent or buy facilities. A short-handled wooden paddle and a few yellow rubber balls were the only equipment necessary.

Platform tennis, which is played on an outdoor, screened-in platform on stilts, was appealing because it required no expensive equipment and no special uniform. It was fun and easy to learn.

Lucie's bubbling enthusiasm made her a popular instructor. Along with volleys and screen shots, she served up a little philosophy. To a group of suburban housewives, she said, "Okay, girls, when you play mixed doubles, don't let your husband intimidate you!

"When he's serving, stand right up at the net in the 'thrust' position. If he tells you to move into the alley and he'll cover the court, *Stand your ground!* Smile at him sweetly and say, 'Dear, this is the way they taught us in clinic. And since you paid the bill, let's try it this way, shall we?' "

After people learned how to play the sport, they wanted to compete. Lucie was instrumental in forming the Metropolitan Area Platform Tennis Association, which sponsors tournaments, as well as men's and women's interclub leagues. Naturally, many of those players wanted advanced lessons.

Lucie began writing informative articles on strokes and strategies for national racquet publications. She participated in exhibitions and tournaments around the Middle Atlantic region. And she had more requests for Paddle, Ltd., clinics than she could schedule.

Today at least half a million Americans play platform tennis. The sport has spread from the East Coast to the Midwest in the winter months. People in Florida, California, and Hawaii play a slightly altered warm-weather version of paddle ball.

The sport has become so popular that Lucie McAvoy no longer has to travel long distances to find a decent game.

She is surrounded by skillful players—many of whom she taught herself.

Lucie still has time for her home, family, and friends. She has earned a high doubles ranking in national tournaments. And she also has a thriving business making profit out of teaching a sport she loves.

10. Making Sports Pay

In the past, sports offered few choices. Career opportunities for women included only teaching, coaching, or playing.

But today the sports business offers an appetizing assortment. Many possible combinations are included in the following chart.

Careers	Employers
1. Adult Fitness	Self; Y's; community centers; fitness clinics; police and fire departments; air lines
2. Senior citizen fitness	Retirement centers and resorts; nursing homes; community centers
3. Military fitness	Army; Navy; Air Force; Marines
4. Infant fitness	Referral from pediatricians
5. Infant education (Perceptual motor)	Day care centers—public, private, universities
6. Industrial fitness	Large corporations
7. Commercial fitness	Self; fitness centers; health spas
8. Cardiac fitness	Self; retirement centers; nursing homes; Y's

CAREERS	EMPLOYERS
9. Cardiac rehabilitation	Y's; medical clinics; established paramedical centers
10. Fitness in space	NASA (Federal Government)
11. Fitness research	Universities; NASA
12. Coaching	Professional teams; public schools
13. Intramural administration/Sports Management	University student unions; penitentiaries; Y's; clubs; professional athletic teams
14. Athletic administration	Professional teams; corporations; clubs; colleges
15. Sports leadership	Community centers; city recreation departments; churches; camps; resorts
16. Commercial sports	Self; established centers—tennis, swim, golf, gymnastics, bowling
17. Sports camps	Self; established sports camps; basketball, football, gymnastics
18. Sports broadcasting	Radio, TV stations
19. Sports journalism	Newspapers; magazines
20. Sports information	Professional athletic teams; colleges and universities
21. Sports photographer	TV stations; newspapers; magazines; teams; self
22. Sports artist	Self; sports magazines
23. Athletic finance	Professional athletic teams; colleges; universities
24. Facilities management	Professional athletic teams; Y's; clubs; agencies; corporations; colleges and universities
25. Sports facilities design	City, county governments; professional athletic teams; private business

Careers	Employers
44. Strength development	Professional athletic teams; college and university athletics
45. Weight control	Self; health spas
46. Sleep clinic (tension control)	Self; established clinics
47. Work analyst	Self; large corporations for physical requirements of various jobs: safety, workman's compensation
48. Sports clothing design; sales	Self; established companies
49. Physical activity for handicapped	Easter Seal; veterans hospitals; state institutions
50. Sports, dance, or fitness for inmates	Penitentiaries

Dr. Charlotte L. Lambert, who is head of the Physical Education Department of Oregon State University, included the above list of Careers and Employers in her article, "What Is Physical Education," which appeared in *JOPER (Journal of Physical Education and Recreation),* May 1980. Reprinted by permission of the author and the publisher.

"The possibilities of using your education to get a good job and to make a good living are endless," says Dr. Lambert. "They are limited only by the way you see yourself and by your definition of physical education."

Dr. Lambert's findings were part of the year-long, government-funded Project ACE (Alliance Career Education), which was sponsored by AAHPERD (American Alliance for Health, Physical Education, Recreation and Dance).

Desks, chairs, and filing cabinets were still being moved into the Washington, D.C., headquarters of Project ACE in November 1978. In the midst of the chaos, directors Carolyn Keith-Henes and Leslie Kiernan discussed plans for the research project.

"We intend to investigate the options—besides coaching and teaching—for careers in physical education and sport," Carolyn said. "First, we will collect information from people all over the country. Then we will develop materials describing the results. We expect that students and teachers—kindergarten through high school—will benefit from this new information on careers."

Two AAPHERD agencies, NAGWS (National Association for Girls and Women in Sport) and NASPE (National Association for Sport and Physical Education) were vitally involved in the project. Would there be a special listing of careers for women?

"No," Leslie said emphatically. "We want to get away from sex-stereotyped roles. The careers are suitable for females as well as males. Sex is no handicap."

In other words, a girl may look at any of the "Ten Career Choices in Physical Education and Sport" (see chart in back of book) and say to herself, "I could do that!"

In November 1979, Project ACE was completed. The desks, chairs, and filing cabinets were moved somewhere else. Carolyn and Leslie had found other projects. But many excellent career guidance materials had resulted. A free pamphlet describing these materials is available from: Career Guidance Materials, AAHPERD Publications (Dept. C), P.O. Box 704, 44 Industrial Park Circle, Waldorf, MD 20601.

Women are already blazing trails in many of the careers listed. "The recreation field was male-oriented in the past," says Daul Valenzuela of Tucson, Arizona. "But today municipalities and federal agencies cannot legally discriminate, so the field is now breaking open for women."

Daul accomplished a big breakthrough herself. She became the first woman to hold the high-level position of Administrator of Parks and Recreation of the City of Tucson.

"My job is to provide a variety of leisure activities to meet the needs of the citizens, from preschoolers to senior citizens," she says. Public relations, park maintenance, hiring, planning, evaluating, and budgeting are all included in her duties.

Daul supervises three coordinators (for sports, cultural arts, and school programs), eleven supervisors, four hundred full-time and up to five hundred summer employees. The facilities under her direction include zoos, golf courses, tennis courts, swimming pools, parks, and recreation centers.

How did she prepare for such a big job? "Well," she says, "I always enjoyed physical activity myself. From the time I was five, I hiked, climbed, and skied in the Adirondack Mountains near my home in New York State. I raised my own horse from a foal and I trained and showed him. I also swam, tumbled, and played softball a lot while I was growing up."

Later Daul earned a degree in recreational education at Cortland State College, which is part of the University of New York. For seven years she worked in the field of recreational therapy in the State Mental Health Department. She married and had three children.

But when her marriage broke up, she decided to tear up her roots and start a new life in the West. Once settled in the beautiful climate of Tucson, she landed a job as cultural arts coordinator for the city. She met and married Ignacio Valenzuela, a Yaqui Indian. Their "tribe" now includes six.

How can she hold this demanding job with such a large family? "My husband gives me a lot of help and support," she explains. "We have an extended family and my mother spends winters here and baby-sits."

Daul's mother is just one of thousands of "snowbirds" who flock to dry, sunny climates each winter. Filling the needs of senior citizens is becoming a larger part of recreational leaders' duties in all parts of the country.

Peggy Weber, who is sports coordinator for the City of Tucson, reports, "They are no longer satisfied with old people's exercise classes. They want to be actively involved. For example, synchronized swimming is really becoming popular with them here."

Peggy also notes trends toward fast-pitch softball and basketball for women as well as coed sports. "We can't form enough coed volleyball leagues to take care of all the teams," she says. "We actually have to turn them away.

"All aspects of leisure activity are expanding incredibly," she continues. "We can't keep up with requests for gymnastics classes since the Olympics. And European sports like soccer are growing faster than football." Peggy feels that increased leisure time, the physical fitness craze, and less frequent moving of families all contribute to the leisure activity boom.

Noting recreational trends and providing programs to fill changing needs are a large part of Peggy's job. And she brought some unusual talents to it. She once trained rodeo horses for barrel jumping. "And I am one of the few women who can drive a stagecoach," she declares with a trace of pride. "With the energy crisis, you never know when that skill might come in handy!"

After earning a degree in secondary education at the University of Arizona, she taught school in Australia, where she also held the intriguing title of "Sports Mistress."

Back home again, she started as a volunteer recreational leader and worked her way up in the Parks and Recreation Department. Today, at thirty, she is the first female to hold the position of sports coordinator for the City of Tucson.

As Peggy's experience shows, becoming an insider as a part- or full-time, paid or volunteer worker can often lead to a good permanent job. By getting a foot in the door, a person has a chance to learn procedures and prove herself. When a regular position becomes available, she will be among the first to know about it and may be hired for a higher salary and more benefits than other applicants.

Interesting jobs with good benefits also exist in the Federal Government. The Civil Service Commission hires recreation, outdoor recreation, therapeutic recreation, and sports specialists. A pamphlet entitled *Recreation Specialist and Related Jobs* (No. AC-504) lists education and experience requirement for these positions.

To qualify for Civil Service grade GS-5, applicants must meet A, B, or C:

    A. Successful completion of a full four-year course of study in an accredited college or university with a major in recreation or therapeutic recreation

B. Three years of experience that demonstrated a knowledge of the goals, tools, principles, methods, and techniques of the field

C. Any equivalent combination of the requirement in A or B

The Civil Service Commission furnishes, without charge, information on federal employment opportunities, qualification requirements, and application procedures.

The address and telephone number of the nearest Federal Job Information Center is listed in local telephone directories (under U.S. Government heading). Or the toll-free telephone number in each state may be obtained by dialing (800) 555-1212.

Private industry also offers promising new employment opportunities. Many corporations are investing in recreational facilities and fitness programs for their employees. They find that fitness programs more than pay for themselves in reduced absenteeism, disability, and lateness and in greater productivity. And these corporations are hiring recreational specialists to direct their programs.

How can girls prepare for these positions? Many choose a recreation major in college. The following three examples show the variety of ways in which different colleges approach this relatively new major.

At the University of Arizona, Dr. Bernard E. Thorn, coordinator of the recreation program, explains that "the primary goal is to prepare students for staff skills and administration responsibility in public and private recreational and group work facilities."

As in many other colleges, the U of A program is under the auspices of the College of Business and Public Administration. Students majoring in Public Recreation Administration develop an emphasis in a specialization, such as therapeutic recreation.

A major in Recreation and Leisure Services at Springfield College in Massachusetts prepares students for "a wide range of dynamic careers working with people," according to the catalog.

The student takes required courses, including dynamic leadership, camp counseling, management of leisure services, public relations in community agencies, economics, and accounting. Then she selects one area of specialization—commercial recreation, community recreation, equestrian arts, resource management, therapeutic recreation, or youth agencies.

Tyler Junior College in Texas is one of the two-year colleges offering a program in recreational leadership. Leading to an Associate in Applied Science degree in recreational leadership, Tyler's program offers "an option in sports facilities management, therapeutic and outdoor recreation designed to present subject matter to acquire the basic knowledge and understanding necessary to organize and supervise a recreation program or community recreational facility."

Careful study of individual college catalogs will acquaint students with possible courses of study in the recreation field.

However, preparation for a career in recreation, physical education, or sports should begin in high school. Subjects such as biology, chemistry, sociology, and other sciences, health, first aid, lifesaving, officiating, and recreational leadership are recommended by AAHPERD.

Participation in sports, whether interscholastic or intramural, is helpful. So is serving as a student team manager, scorekeeper, trainer, reporter, photographer, or official. Taking part in a work-study or teacher-aide program can provide valuable experience, as can volunteering to assist in a community recreational program.

Experience and education are not the only effective keys to open doors in the sports business, however. Many women use enterprise and ingenuity.

Laura O'Rourke, for instance, was a psychiatric nurse before she became a women's sports retailer. She recognized a need in her community—and she filled it.

"I had to drive a half hour to buy a leotard for my gymnast daughter," she explains. "One day I thought to myself, Why doesn't somebody open a leotard shop nearby, in fact, why don't I?"

During several months of market research, she discovered

that her area, Summit, New Jersey, had a number of dance schools and a YMCA that offered forty-eight classes a week that required leotards.

Today she carries a large inventory of dance apparel and shoes as well as a variety of sports fashions in her store, The Female Athlete.

LeAnne Schreiber was at Harvard preparing for a career teaching English literature when the idea of becoming a journalist first hit her. Who would believe that just four years later she would hold the biggest single job in sports journalism—sports editor of *The New York Times*?

"One day I wrote a letter to the editor at *Time* magazine listing ideas that I thought would make good stories," she recalls. "He hired me on the spot—to write about international politics." Later, she asked for an assignment to cover the 1976 Montreal Olympics. She wrote three cover-length stories in three weeks, even though she had never written a single sports story before.

As a result of those stories, *Women's Sports* magazine offered her the job of editor. After a "blissful" year and a half running the magazine, she moved on to accept the job of assistant sports editor of *The New York Times*. Then, at thirty-three, she made history when she became the first female sports editor of that traditionally male-dominated newspaper, in 1978.

LeAnne, Laura, Peggy, Daul, Carolyn, Leslie, and Charlotte are just a few of the thousands of women across the country who are enjoying an assortment of challenging careers in the broad field of physical education, recreation, and sports.

11. Playing Through a Lifetime

Athletes used to pack their sportsgear in mothballs once their school days were past. They traded their hockey sticks and track shoes for bleachers and armchairs.

But today, all across the country, Americans are getting out of their armchairs. They are starting sports earlier and enjoying them longer. They are playing all through their lifetimes.

For example:

In Des Moines, Iowa, ten leotarded ladies cancel their garden club meeting to attend aerobic dancing class.

In Dunedin, Florida, four gray-haired widows abandon the bridge table to try out a grandson's new basketball hoop.

In Orono, Maine, two teenagers switch off *Monday Night Football* to jog a mile in the moonlight.

Suddenly the roads across America are filled with joggers, bicyclists, and roller skaters. Racquetball courts and bowling alleys are booked solid. And people who were too tired to carry out the garbage are eagerly signing up for weight-lifting programs.

The physical fitness boom has hit. But will it go out of style like hula hoops and mini-skirts? Or will it last?

Odds are that it will last. Americans see the need to conserve their best natural resource—their own bodies.

"Start young!" advises the President's Council on Physical Fitness and Sports. This Council was created within the parent agency, AAHPERD (American Alliance for Health, Physical Education, Recreation and Dance). In 1966 it began a national award system designed to help measure and motivate the fitness of boys and girls.

In schools and youth groups across the nation, people aged ten to seventeen are tested on performance of six items in the AAHPERD Youth Fitness Test and compared to national standards. Those who score at or above the 85th percentile receive a special certificate and a red, white, and blue emblem. So far, over five million girls and boys have earned the right to wear the Presidential Physical Fitness Award.

In addition to starting fitness programs young, children may now begin sports programs at an earlier age than they used to. In many school systems, fourth grade has become standard instead of junior or senior high school.

Team sports continue to be popular. Cooperative, "everybody plays" sports like soccer and volleyball are gaining favor.

But the newest trend is toward lifetime sports. Schools and colleges are beginning to emphasize them in athletic programs. As the term implies, these sports can be played throughout life, during and long after school years.

They can be played at many levels of skill. In skiing, the novice can have as much fun on the slopes as the expert. In racquetball, the Class C player can get as much exercise as the Class A.

Lifetime sports are individual. For most of them, one needs few other people. Unlike the basketball player, who needs nine others for a game, the tennis player needs only one. The swimmer, runner, or bicyclist can even choose to go it alone.

Cooperative, "everybody plays" sports like volleyball are gaining in popularity

Montgomery Newspapers

The lifetime sports can be approached from a variety of angles. They can be played competitively or casually, for fun or for profit. Or all of the above. Golf is a good example.

An outstanding golfer like Cathy Hanlon, of Palos Verdes Estates, California, has three options—she can be an amateur player, a teaching professional, or a playing professional.

At nineteen, Cathy has the world at the end of her putter. Ever since she played her first tournament at the age of twelve, she was one of the top junior golfers in Southern California, which is a highly competitive area. She consistently scored well in local, state, and national events. Winning the Los Angeles City Junior Championships at sixteen and seventeen were among the highlights of her career.

One of her proudest moments came in 1978 when she was seventeen. She was named the All-American Girl Junior Golfer of the Year by the American Junior Golf Association.

"This was a thrill, because the award was announced at a huge banquet and I had to make a speech," Kathy smiles. "What made me so proud was that the award meant that I was the number one junior girl golfer in the country."

Another high point came at nineteen, when she won the Los Angeles City Women's Championships, after placing second the two years preceding. As the winner, she was thrilled to receive the same trophy that Babe Didrikson had won in 1944.

But golf has not been all victories, trophies, and banquets for Cathy. "I've had a few big disappointments," she admits. "I think my loss to Carol Semple in the quarterfinals of the 1980 U.S. Amateur stands out the most because it was recent.

"It was a hard loss. I was two up with three to go and then one up on the last hole. I missed a short putt on the last hole and also on the second play-off hole to lose the match. What made it so disappointing is that I worked so hard and I was leading practically the whole way. Luckily I learned a lot from the whole thing!"

On the bright side, what is she getting from golf? "First of

Women's softball teams are forming rapidly in Tucson

Dave Fonda

all, I'm getting a free education at Southern Methodist University in Dallas," she says. When she returns for her sophomore
year, she will again play one of the top two positions on a team
that ranked No. 2 in the 1980 nationals.

"Second, I'm getting the opportunity to travel and make
friends all over the country. Because of this travel, I have
acquired responsibility and the ability to handle many things
on my own. Lately, I have learned to discipline myself when
necessary.

"It is difficult to combine studying with the golf tournaments," she explains. "But I have learned that it's a matter of
training your mind to concentrate on certain things at certain
times."

Cathy has had to make sacrifices because of her golf, "mostly
in the social area." She advises other women to follow in her
cleated footsteps only if they are willing to make the sacrifices
that golf demands.

"It takes a lot of time and an extremely dedicated person,"
she says. "But I feel that the rewards of participating in golf
more than make up for the sacrifices."

Will she turn pro? "Not yet," she declares. "I want to finish
college first. I'm a physical education major. Playing on the
college golf team is good experience for me—the competition
is excellent!

"My hopes for the years ahead are to achieve the goals I have
set for myself in golf and also to parallel these goals with the
ones I have made for myself in life. In other words, I'd like to
play professional golf, but at the same time not make it my
whole life."

Some female golfers choose instead to compete in the Group
Fore Mini-Tour of the WPGT (Women's Professional Golf
Tour). This tour attracts young women who are reluctant or

unable to attend college or cannot afford to compete in the big amateur tournaments. It is open to any woman golfer, amateur or pro, who is eighteen years or older and has an 8 or better handicap.

The tour serves as a sort of prep school for the Ladies Professional Golf Association (LPGA) circuit. Since its beginning in

1975, the Mini-Tour has been the first and only developmental tour in the United States for women's professional golf. It is designed to offer competitive experience to women golfers who seek a career in professional golf as a touring pro. Amateurs with low handicaps also play the WPGT.

Professionals compete for tournament purses ranging from $2,500 to $10,000. In 1978, the average purse was $4,000. The WPGT has two series per year, both extending from one LPGA qualifying school to the next.

If Cathy should choose to turn professional and play the LPGA tour, she would first have to attend qualifying school. The basic requirements for tournament status are as follows:

1. Applicants must be at least eighteen years of age, or have special permission from the Commissioner to petition for membership.
2. Applicants must have an approved and authenticated USGA (U.S. Golf Association) handicap of 3 or better.
3. Application must be accompanied by two letters from recognized golf professionals as to the player's tournament ability at the time of application to the school.
4. Applicants must be able to show proper financial responsibility for maintenance on tour as determined by Commissioner and Player Council.

Once a member of the LPGA Tournament Division after completing the school, a player must meet certain performance guidelines. An apprentice member must participate in twelve LPGA cosponsored or approved official tournaments each year (Class B, ten; Class A, ten; international members, six). Her first year as a member, she must earn a minimum $2,500 in total official money and $4,800 each subsequent year. A member playing in fewer than ten tournaments must average $300 per tournament.

Of course, Cathy might not top Nancy Lopez' record earnings of $189,813.83 in her rookie year, 1978. But the financial possibilities are definitely appealing.

Money in women's golf has increased dramatically in the last twenty-five years. In 1956, LPGA purses totaled $140,447; in 1979, $4,400,000. And the winner's share became worth the effort of perfecting a chip shot.

In the 1956 Women's U.S. Open Championships, for example, winner Kathy Cornelius took home $1,500 from a $6,000 purse. In the same event in 1978, Hollis Stacy won $15,000 from a $100,000 purse. The number of tournaments also jumped—from twenty-six in 1956 to thirty-eight in 1979.

The touring pros often earn extra income in other ways—by lending their names and expertise to golf schools, or by becoming product representatives for manufacturers of sporting goods and clothing, or by endorsing unrelated items such as fruit juice or toothpaste.

A golfer might choose instead to become a teaching professional—like Jan Van Munching.

Jan, a tall, attractive brunette, is a teaching pro at the new No. 6 course at the world-famous Pinehurst Country Club in North Carolina. She came to Pinehurst right after graduating from Mt. Holyoke College, where she captained the golf team for three years.

"Playing football and baseball with my five brothers toughened me up," Jan laughs. "I learned to compete." Now she teaches golf to men as well as women in clinics and private lessons.

"A female pro is still a novelty," she says. "But I'm finding that many women relate better to another woman. Our anatomy is different from a man's. So we have to swing differently."

Jan's ambition is to be a head pro. To reach her goal, she must work her way through the LPGA Teaching Division from apprentice, to Class B, to Class A. "Application for membership is open to female teachers of golf and country clubs, approved driving ranges, approved golf organizations and other persons exceptionally qualified and actively involved with golf instruction, leadership and service," according to LPGA pamphlets.

A low handicap is not enough. An applicant must pass written and practical examinations at each step. She must know about golf rules, teaching golf, golf shop operations, merchandising, golf course operations and maintenance, golf car operations and maintenance, and old and new terminology.

Applications, reference materials, and further information are available from the Ladies Professional Golf Association, 919 Third Avenue, New York, NY 10022.

Not everyone wants to make a career out of a lifetime sport. Many people simply enjoy the exercise, companionship, and personal satisfaction the sport offers.

For women like Jane McCullough Hamilton, sixty-nine, of Rydal, Pennsylvania, those rewards are enough. "I've been playing amateur golf for over fifty years," Jane declares. "And I still love it."

To show for those years, she has scrapbooks full of clippings describing her victories. "The papers printed lots of stories and pictures of amateur players back in the '30s," she says. "Now all they care about is the professionals." She has drawers full of contestant's badges commemorating the many times she played in the Women's National Amateur Championships. And she has shelves full of trophies for winning her club championship uncountable times over a forty-year period.

"Even more important, I have friendships I've made all across the country through golf," she says.

Jane also has a trim athletic figure, a youthful tanned face, and a stylish blond hairdo streaked by the sun. The above-the-knee brilliant yellow, pink, and green golf outfit she wears today is a great contrast to the below-the-knee, plain pastel dresses she used to wear in the 1920's and '30s. "My mother was horrified when I wanted to wear shorts in those days," she laughs. "She made me pass bending-over inspection before I could leave for the golf course!"

Her teammates at Huntingdon Valley Country Club declare that today her swing is as good as it ever was. She began learning that winning swing when she was just ten years old.

"We lived on a farm," she reminisces. "My mother and father were avid golfers. And my older brother, 'Duff' McCullough, became one of the top national amateurs. I had two choices: I could stay home and play with the horses and dogs

Jane McCullough in 1930 and as she appears today on the same golf course

and chickens, or I could play golf with them. I played golf!"

Jane entered her first tournament at eleven and later won the Junior Championships of Philadelphia at fifteen and sixteen. Since the only "athletic activity" her all-girl school offered was military drill, she happily got herself excused to play golf. As a teenager she played on the ladies' team of her country club.

"My best years were the late '20s and early '30s," she says. "I was runner-up in the Philadelphia Women's Championship when I was eighteen and again when I was twenty-two. And I won my club championship for the first time when I was nineteen."

When she married, her mother warned, "You'd better keep up your golf or you'll be left home." Jane has been glad she heeded this advice, for she has enjoyed golf on business trips with her husband all around the country. And she has never been left home on a Sunday.

127

Not even the birth of three boys could keep her from the course. "I hardly missed a team match for a pregnancy," she chuckles.

In the 1930's, Jane's handicap was 3 or 4. Today, fifty years later, it has only climbed to 12. She plays two or three times a week on her home course and every day while vacationing at Bald Peak Colony Club, New Hampshire, or Delray, Florida. And she competes in the senior women's national tournaments to this day.

At sixty-nine, Jane McCullough Hamilton says, "I like to win a match. But mainly I just like to play well. Golf gives me exercise and friends and travel. I never want to give it up!"

At nineteen, Cathy Hanlon puts it this way, "I figure I can't always play softball. But I can *always* play golf!"

Is golf the best lifetime sport? Or is tennis, swimming, rowing, bicycling, running, skiing, racquetball, skating, bowling, or squash? Players of these sports may violently disagree on the answer to this question. But they all do agree on one piece of advice: "Start young!"

12. Blazing Trails

A sportswoman today is a trailblazer. She is greeted by new rewards at each turn. And she leaves her marks for others to follow.

Beginning in the 1970's, television brought sportswomen to the world's attention. "Female athletes are worth watching" became an exciting new concept. The new sports heroines not only entertained millions of viewers, they inspired and informed them as well.

> After Olga Korbut stunned eight hundred million worldwide viewers with her gymnastic performance in the 1972 Munich Olympics, the number of female gymnasts in the United States alone increased from 15,000 to 50,000 in two years.

> When Billie Jean King trounced Bobby Riggs in the famous "Battle of the Sexes" tennis match in 1973, she proved that women can compete with men in sports—and win.

> When Nancy Lopez won an unprecedented fifth-straight tournament in her rookie year on the women's golf tour, men and women alike studied her classic swing in order to improve their own.

And millions cheered when Janet Guthrie became the first female driver in the Indianapolis 500, and when seventeen-year-old Chris Evert toppled the greats at Wimbledon, and when a filly named Genuine Risk won the 1980 Kentucky Derby.

These athletes are all trailblazers. Perhaps others will follow who are faster, stronger, or braver. But not even time can fade the joy that comes from knowing: "I got here first!"

There are many ways to be first. Some women like to break records; others like to break down the barriers of tradition.

Many a sportsgirl today feels like a weary backpacker who suddenly comes upon a cool mountain pond—only to find it posted: BOYS ONLY—GIRLS KEEP OUT. She tears down the sign and plunges in. She believes she has the right to swim, too.

Such a courageous girl was Maria Pepe. Maria was a pigtailed twelve-year-old who wanted to play Little League Baseball in 1972. In her tryout with the Hoboken, New Jersey, team, she proved she was qualified. The local team enrolled her, but the national headquarters of Little League overruled: "Boys only."

Maria was not about to go home and play with Barbie dolls. She believed she had every right to play baseball. Her parents agreed with her, so they took her case to the New Jersey Civil Rights Division.

For five days, arguments raged back and forth about the differences between boys and girls in muscle strength. In the end, no definite proof could be offered that boys excelled over girls in this area, at least between the ages of eight and twelve!

The hearing officer ruled that Little League was practicing discrimination on the basis of sex. Perhaps one sentence in the decision should be posted in all male locker rooms:

> The sooner little boys begin to realize that there are many areas in life in which girls are their equal and that it is no great shame, no great burden to be bested by a girl, then perhaps we come that much closer to the legislative ideal of sexual equality as well as relieving a source of emotional difficulty for men.

Sportsgirls today are indebted to trailblazer Maria Pepe,
the first female Little Leaguer

Dave Fonda

Men can learn something from watching Lori Castello's classic swing

Montgomery Newspapers

Little League, "a public accommodation," was ordered to admit girls to full membership in 1974. Maria won her case and her turn at bat. Girls all over America can share the rewards from the victory of one brave girl.

Some girls dare to plunge into sports that have traditionally been thought "too dangerous" for females—like horse racing. Only since 1969 have females been allowed to receive jockey licenses. But given the chance, they have scored thousands of victories at tracks all over the country.

Rochelle Lee, for example, is one of the best female jockeys in the United States, according to Frank Sammarco, the jockey director at Keystone Race Track in Cornwells Heights, Pennsylvania.

The tiny (4'11", 98-pound) twenty-three-year-old Rochelle has also earned the respect and admiration of other jockeys, trainers, owners, and fans alike.

Today, for the first race at Keystone, she is mounted on No. 11, a big dark-brown mare named Espy May. Rochelle is a colorful figure in a powder-blue jacket, emblazoned with an orange sunburst, white nylon pants, and long black boots. Her long blond hair is tucked under a pale-blue cap.

The track is her stage. It is set with masses of red and white flowers, sculptured bushes, sparkling fountains and lakes. A huge electronic tote board records the constantly changing betting odds for the first race.

Along with eleven other jockeys, Rochelle rides her horse slowly toward the starting gate at the far side of the track.

Does she know that the odds are now 6–1 on her? Is she calculating her share of the purse for win, place, or show? Is she worried about another accident? Or is she simply concentrating on getting the best possible performance out of the horse?

Whatever her thoughts may be, they are cut short. The bell rings. They're off.

Suddenly Rochelle and Espy May are lost in a sea of brilliant silks and gleaming horses thundering down the track and around the turn. She bends low over the horse's neck and urges her on. Twice she uses the whip and they spurt forward.

Nearing the finish line, they hold the lead for an instant, but then one horse inches ahead and then another. The race is over. Number 11 is third.

Rochelle is weary and spattered with mud as she enters the female jockeys' room. But her smile is broad.

"My horse was trying as hard as she could," she says. "That's the most I could ask." Then she sprawls in an armchair

"The more you ride, the stronger you get," says Rochelle
Lee. "And the stronger you get, the more you win"
Courtesy of Keystone Race Track

to study her own performance in a slow-motion rerun on
closed-circuit television.

"I'm always trying to improve," she declares. "I never stop
learning—and the only way to learn is from experience." Rochelle now has five years of racing experience and scores of
wins to her credit. She is so much in demand that she often
rides five races in a single afternoon.

But she recognizes that getting started and gaining experience is very difficult, especially for a girl. Many trainers refuse
to hire girls, mainly because they believe they lack the strength
to pull the horse's head up.

"I can't think of any job that would suit me better than being a jockey," says Rochelle Lee

Courtesy of Keystone Race Track

"But it's like a merry-go-round," Rochelle argues, "The more you ride, the stronger you get; and the stronger you get, the more you win; and the more you win, the more you ride."

So how does a girl climb aboard this merry-go-round?

"The trick is to find a trainer who likes girl jockeys and is willing to give them a chance." she says. "I was lucky—I was in the right place at the right time."

For her, the right place and time were a racetrack in Bowie, Maryland, in 1974, the year she graduated from high school. A trainer there gave her a chance and a contract.

But luck was not the only factor. Rochelle had already spent years preparing for this opportunity. Growing up in West Virginia, she had learned to ride at the stables of a friend. By fourteen, she was riding ponies and jumpers in the horse-show circuit. And by sixteen, she was teaching riding every morning

135

before school and working out every afternoon. But what she really wanted to do was race.

At the Bowie racetrack, she learned to "breeze" horses to prepare them for races. She studied slow-motion race films. And she mastered a special skill—the ability to whip either right- or left-handed.

After winning a few races in West Virginia and Maryland, she got her next big break. She was hired to ride a horse at the newly opened Keystone Race Track, and she won her first race!

Rochelle's blue eyes open wide with that happy memory. "If you have the horse, you'll win," she declares modestly. "It's ninety percent horse and ten percent rider."

Getting good horses to ride became easier and easier the more she won. Soon she was so much in demand that she hired an agent to take care of her bookings. And she raced at many tracks in addition to Keystone.

When she began racing, she had "bugs," the asterisks in the racing form which signify allowances for an inexperienced jockey. But today, she is "bugless," which means she is a full-fledged jockey.

Rochelle is willing to work hard at her profession. Every morning except Sunday, from 6 to 10 she is at the track exercising horses, no matter whether the thermometer reads 20°F below or 90°F above. She then goes home to her nearby apartment or falls asleep on a bunk in the jockey room. At noon she starts getting ready for the afternoon races, which run every day but Thursday. "The only time a race is canceled is if the track is frozen," she says. "I've ridden in snow, rain, lightning, and thunder!"

Is racing dangerous? "I don't think about that," she says. "Although I did have a bad accident three years ago— the horses were bunched . . . my horse fell and broke both front legs . . . other horses fell, too. I had compressed vertebrae, a smashed nose, fractured eye socket, crushed cheekbone. I was out of racing for eight months. But I'm fine now!" As proof, she wrinkles her pug nose and grins broadly.

"I figure if an accident's going to happen, it will. You can't be too cautious in this business," she believes.

"The best part is that I get to be around horses," says
Rochelle Lee

Courtesy of Keystone Race Track

Now she is putting on clean white pants and a gold-and-black jacket for the next race. As she pulls on her high boots, she looks up and adds, "I really like being a jockey. I can't think of any other job that could give me so much—I have money in the bank, I have the fans, the excitement of the races. And best of all, I get to be around horses. That's worth taking a few risks!"

Then she adjusts her gold cap, and she's off.

Courage to take risks seems to be a common quality among trailblazing sportswomen. Elaine Perkins, for instance, risked everything she owned to break into a career in television broadcasting.

"I sold my furniture, packed all my worldly goods into my car, and set off to find a job," she remembers. "I didn't have enough experience for an impressive résumé. So I decided to start in Seattle and work my way down the coast, just knocking on doors."

To her amazement, the first door opened. She arrived in Seattle on New Year's Day 1977, and has not left since. In two days she landed a job at KING-TV, Channel 5, and became Seattle's first female sportscaster.

Currently Elaine anchors the sports portion of the weekend news at 5:30 and 11 P.M., as well as other programs scattered throughout the week. She produces her own shows and does all the interviewing, editing, and scriptwriting.

Her straightforward delivery has won the approval of the viewers. "I want to get rid of the giggly, brainless image of *some* female sportscasters," she declares, mentioning a well-known name.

"The people of Seattle have been wonderfully patient with me," she adds. "These two and a half years have been a learning experience for my audience as well as for me."

Through the week, she does field reporting for special sports feature "packages." In order to do "color commentary," she often travels with various teams, such as the Seattle SuperSonics basketball team and the Washington State football team. During her speaking engagements around the state, the question always arises, "What about the men's locker rooms?"

"Oh, the guys used to be shocked to see me there," she answers with a laugh. "But they are getting more casual about it now. They either get dressed or wrap up in a towel. We're so informal they sometimes even pass me their hand lotion while we're talking. They're getting used to having me around —they know they'll see me again.

"When I do postgame interviews, I ask for particular players," she explains. "They can come out of the locker room or invite me in. They respect the fact that I honor their wishes."

The locker room is just one of the many challenges Elaine has conquered along her path. The first came when the editor of her Marion (Ohio) high school newspaper flatly declared, "Girls don't write about sports—only boys do!"

She felt personally insulted, but she persisted. Finally the right opportunity came up. "None of the boys wanted to keep on writing about a losing football team," she recalls. "So I got the assignment."

Encouraged by her "sports nut" father, she studied rule books and sports pages until she knew her subject well. At Ohio State, she majored in journalism and later wrote free-lance sports articles.

After moving to Los Angeles, she seized another opportunity. KFWB, the news radio station, was holding a "Women's Equality Day," during which female celebrities read the news. Since no celebrity was available to do the sports, Elaine once again got the job. "Afterward, I convinced all my friends to send in postcards saying how great I was," she now confesses. "And the station kept me on part time."

But she still had the itch to move on to television. So she hired an acting coach to work with her for several months. Then she landed a job at a small television station in Bakersfield, California, to gain experience. She could only survive the desert heat for four months before she decided to make the job-hunting tour that landed her in Seattle.

During the past several years, Elaine has seen the interest in women's sports increasing. Yet coverage is still limited mostly to personality features rather than news. "For the most part,

Interviewing superathletes such as Reggie Jackson is just part of the job of Seattle's first female TV sportscaster, Elaine Perkins

KING Broadcasting

women don't yet know how to get publicity," she says. "They need more experience in recognizing the needs of the media and making the proper approach."

Perhaps they should take a leaf out of Elaine Perkins' plan book. She has used intelligence, persistence, hard work, and a good bit of daring to achieve the goals along her path.

Whether or not her achievements are recorded in video highlights or newspaper headlines, every sportswoman should realize that she is a vital soldier in the continuing battle for equal opportunity. For unknowns and superstars alike, every victory counts.

And every sportswoman can contribute. The way Karen

Fielding and Abby Myers did, for example. Karen and Abby were two freshmen at Madison (New Jersey) High School who simply wanted the opportunity to play good tennis.

"The school let us try out for the boys' tennis team, since there was no girls' team," Abby remembers. "After playing challenge matches, we won two out of the eleven spots on the team. We both won every league match we played, even though all of the opponents were boys."

Did Abby and Karen really prefer to compete against boys? No. They simply wanted a chance to play their sport against good competition. They had no other choice—the boys' league was "the only game in town."

And later, they scored their biggest victory—for their younger sisters as well as themselves—because the next year the school started a girls' tennis team! There were no newspaper headlines for Karen and Abby, but they were trailblazers, nevertheless.

Today there are thousands of courageous sportswomen like Karen and Abby, Kim and Debbie, Rochelle and Elaine. In cities, towns, and suburbs all around the world, they are eager to explore the forest of sports.

The women's liberation movement, new legislation, and the physical fitness boom have helped to clear the way. But each girl must have the courage, dedication, and grit to forge ahead.

For sportsgirls everywhere, the time is right to tighten shoelaces, straighten shoulders, and take the first step.

Afterword

Many agencies are ready and willing to assist female athletes. People in national organizations provided information generously. I am particularly grateful to the Amateur Athletic Union of the U.S., Inc., the American Alliance for Health, Physical Education, Recreation and Dance (especially Project ACE), the Association of Intercollegiate Athletics for Women, the Ladies Professional Golf Association, the National Ski Patrol, the United States Tennis Association, the United States Olympic Committee, and the Women's Equity Action League Educational and Legal Defense Fund.

Publications such as *The New York Times, The Philadelphia Inquirer, The* (Philadelphia) *Bulletin,* and the Montgomery Newspapers provided day-to-day news of the expanding sports picture for girls. Their increasing coverage is added proof that "female athletes are worth watching."

Further Information

Advisory Council for Camps
400 Madison Avenue
New York, NY 10017
*(Free service for locating suitable camps
for children and teenagers)*

**Amateur Athletic Union of the
    U.S., Inc.**
AAU House
3400 West 86th Street
Indianapolis, IN 46268

**Amateur Basketball Association
    of the U.S.A. (USOC)***
1750 Boulder Street
Colorado Springs, CO 80909

**American Alliance for Health,
    Physical Education, Recreation
    and Dance (AAHPERD)**
1900 Association Drive
Reston, VA 22091

**American Canoe Association
    (USOC)**
P.O. Box 248
Lorton, VA 22079

**American Fencers League of
    America (USOC)**
601 Curtis Street

Albany, CA 94706

**American Horse Shows
    Association (USOC)**
598 Madison Avenue
New York, NY 10022

**Aquatics Division of the AAU
    (Swimming, Diving,
    Synchronized Swimming)
    (USOC)**
AAU House
3400 West 86th Street
Indianapolis, IN 46268

**Association for Intercollegiate
    Athletics for Women**
1201 16th Street, N.W.
Washington, DC 20036

**Athletics—Track and Field
    Division of the AAU (USOC)**
AAU House
3400 West 86th Street
Indianapolis, IN 46268

Center for Women and Sport
Pennsylvania State University
White Building
University Park, PA 16802

**Education and Research Center of
    the United States Tennis
    Association**

---

*United States Olympic Committee governing body

145

729 Alexander Road
Princeton, NJ 08540

**Eldora Outdoor Recreation for the
Disabled**
Box 430
Nederland, CO 80466

**Ladies Professional Golf
Association**
919 Third Avenue
New York, NY 10022

**Luge Division of the AAU
(USOC)**
AAU House
3400 West 86th Street
Indianapolis, IN 46268

**National Archery Association of
the United States (USOC)**
1750 East Boulder Street
Colorado Springs, CO 80909

**National Association of Amateur
Oarsmen (USOC)**
4 Boathouse Row
Philadelphia, PA 19130

**National Association for Girls
and Women in Sport**
1900 Association Drive
Reston, VA 22091

**National Athletic Trainers
Association**
Business Office
112 South Pitt Street
P.O. Drawer 1865
Greenville, NC 27834

**National Collegiate Athletic
Association**
U.S. Highway 50 and Nall Avenue
P.O. Box 1906
Shawnee Mission, KS 66222

National Jogging Association
919 18th Street, N.W., Suite 830
Washington, DC 20006

**National Rifle Association of
America (USOC)**

1600 Rhode Island Avenue, N.W.
Washington, DC 20036

National Ski Patrol®System, Inc.
2901 Sheridan Boulevard
Denver, CO 80214

Nick Bollittieri Tennis Academy
Colony Beach and Tennis Resort
1620 Gulf of Mexico Drive
Longboat Key, FL 33548

Office for Civil Rights
U.S. Department of Education
Washington, DC 20201

Parkette Gymnastic Camp
Lehigh Valley Gymnastic Training
Center
10 Juniper Road AO
Macungie, PA 18062

**President's Council on Physical
Fitness and Sports**
Room 3030 6th Street, S.W.
Washington, DC 20101

> **Fitness test materials**
> AAHPERD Publications (Dept.
> BB)
> P.O. Box 704
> 44 Industrial Park Circle
> Waldorf, MD 20601

**Professional Ski Instructors of
America**
2015 South Pontiac Way, Suite 1A
Denver, CO 80224

**United States Field Hockey
Association (USOC)**
4415 Buffalo Road
N. Chili, NY 14514

**United States Figure Skating
Association**
Sears Crescent Building
500 City Hall Plaza
Boston, MA 02108

**United States Gymnastics
Federation (USOC)**
P.O. Box 12713

4545 East 5th Street
Tucson, AZ 85732

**United States International
Skating Association (USOC—
speed skating)**
Beggs Mainland Drive
Oconomowoc, WI 53066

**United States Olympic
Committee**
Training Center-Colorado Springs
1776 East Boulder Street
Colorado Springs, CO 80909

**United States Professional Tennis
Association**
6701 Highway 58
Harrison, TN 37341

**United States Ski Association
(USOC)**
1726 Champa Street, Suite 300
Denver, CO 80202

**United States Team Handball
Federation (USOC)**
10 Nottingham Road
Short Hills, NJ 07078

**United States Tennis Association
(USOC)**
51 East 42d Street
New York, NY 10017

**United States Volleyball
Association (USOC)**
P.O. Box 77065
San Francisco, CA 94107

U.S. Yacht Racing Union (USOC)
820 Davis Street
Evanston, IL 60201

**Women's Equity Action League
Educational and Legal Defense
Fund (WEAL Fund)**
805 15th Street, N.W., Suite 822
Washington, DC 20005

Women's Professional Golf Tour
10431 Lockwood Drive
Cupertino, CA 95014

Women's Sports Foundation
195 Moulton Street
San Francisco, CA 94123

Women's Tennis Association
1604 Union Street
San Francisco, CA 94123

Date

Director, Office for Civil Rights
U.S. Department of Education
Washington, DC 20201

Dear Director:

I am (We are) hereby filing a complaint of sex discrimination (and race or national origin discrimination, if applicable) against______________________________________(name and address of the institution). This discrimination violates Title IX of the Education Amendments of 1972 and other applicable laws.[1]

The name(s) and address(es) of the person(s) filing this complaint is (are)[2]:

____

The person (people) hurt by the sex discrimination is (are)[3]:

____

A description of the sex discrimination I am (we are) complaining about follows[4]:

____

____

I (We) hereby request an immediate investigation of this complaint and notification of the dates it is to take place. I (We) also request copies of all written preliminary findings of the investigation and of the specific facts upon which such findings are based and a copy of all of your agency's correspondence with the institution pertaining to your determination with respect to the complaint as to whether a violation has occurred.

Sincerely,

____
(Signature)

Name
Address
Telephone Number

cc[5]

INSTRUCTIONS

1. If employment discrimination is involved, other federal, state, and local fair employment laws may also be violated. This letter can be modified to serve as a complaint under Executive Order 11246, Title VII of the 1964 Civil Rights Act, the Equal Pay Act of 1963, or Title VIII of the Public Health Service Act.

2. The complainant need not be the person discriminated against, and indeed an individual is probably afforded greater protection against possible harassment or retaliation if a group files on behalf of that individual.

3. Fill in the names and addresses of the persons discriminated against if three or fewer persons. If there are more than three persons, describe them in general. For example, "the part-time faculty members in the College of Arts and Sciences," "the female members of the ski team," or "all the girls in the sixth-grade class."

4. Describe what the institution has done that is discriminatory; the approximate dates when the discrimination took place; whether the discrimination is still continuing; identify by name any persons who were the ones who discriminated and describe their position or relationship to the institution; describe how the discrimination took place; and provide some details to explain what happened that was discriminatory. If the discrimination is causing an emergency such as the loss of a job, explain the emergency and *underline* it. Attach some of the evidence you have, such as copies of letters or memoranda which you want to provide. Before the investigation begins, you can submit additional information.

5. Suggestion: Unless you want to preserve your confidentiality, send copies of your complaint, without the evidence, to persons with influence on eliminating discrimination. It can be useful to show on the complaint that you sent copies as follows:

   cc: Title IX Coordinator and/or Equal Opportunity Officer
       U.S. senators and representatives from the state or district where the institution is located
       Governor
       Selected state legislators
       Campus, state, or local commission on the status of women
       State or local human rights commission
       Student and faculty governing bodies
       Alumni organizations
       Organizations and projects like WEAL Fund and PEER
       Local chapters of national women's organizations like WEAL and NOW
       Women's caucus of the appropriate professional society
       Local and/or state newspapers, with a brief press release describing the action you are taking
       SPRINT—805 15th Street, N.W., Washington, DC 20005 (#822)

149

Athletic Trainer

Works in schools and colleges or with professional teams in prevention and care of injuries. *Preparation:* College, in curriculum approved by the National Certification Examination. *Compensation:* Schools—$7,000–$12,000; Pro teams —$12,000–$25,000. *Job Outlook:* Good.

Sports Official

Employed by schools, colleges, sport clubs, and recreation departments to conduct athletic contests in all sports. May be eligible for assignment to professional contests. *Preparation:* Training and qualifying examination in each sport. Must hold membership in officials' organization for each sport. *Compensation:* Clubs, schools, recreation departments—$10–$50 per contest; Professional—$50–$500 per contest. *Job Outlook:* Good.

Professional Athlete

Plays baseball, football, basketball, hockey, softball, track and field, tennis, golf, skates or bowls before paying audiences. *Preparation:* High school, college for most sports. Intensive coaching and practice. *Compensation:* $2,500–$100,000. *Job Outlook:* Very few opportunities, heavy competition.

Recreation Leader

Organizes and directs leisure activities in public agencies, parks, and institutions and corporations. Supervises part-time and volunteer workers. *Preparation:* 2–4 year college degree in recreation and/or related fields. *Compensation:* $7,500–$15,000. *Job Outlook:* Fair.

Physical Education Teacher

Prepares lesson plans and tests, works with students evaluating skills, sportsmanship, effort, and participation, preschool through adult levels. *Preparation:* College degrees and appropriate teaching credentials. *Compensation:* $8,000–$25,000. *Job Outlook:* Fair.

Athletic Coach

Coaches team or individual sports. May specialize in one sport or one aspect of a sport plan, organize practice sessions and strategy. May teach P.E., health, or other subjects; business arrangements, press interviews. In schools, colleges, community and professional sports. *Preparation:* College degree with credits in physical education, education and coaching techniques. *Compensation:* $300 (part-time) to $75,000+. *Job Outlook:* Excellent for part-time, fair for full-time.

Sports Journalist or Photographer

Works with all media in interpreting the sports world to the public. Opportunities exist at local or big-city newspapers, TV, radio stations, magazines, at colleges or universities. *Preparation:* College degree with credits in communications. Sports experience helpful. Photography experience. *Compensation:* $6,000–$30,000. *Job Outlook:* Good.

Sporting Goods Dealer
Sells sporting goods or manages a department or store. Supervises purchasing and marketing, office and sales personnel. May represent a manufacturer. *Preparation:* College degree or management training programs. Sports experience helpful. *Compensation:* $9,000–$25,000+. *Job Outlook:* Excellent.

Physical Therapist
Works with physically disabled. Evaluates physiological functions and selects therapeutic procedures. *Preparation:* College degree and state licensing. *Compensation:* $8,000–$25,000. *Job Outlook:* Good.

Physical Education and/or Athletic Administrator
Organizes and supervises competitive and/or instructional programs in clubs, schools, colleges, and professional sports. Responsible for transportation, budget, facilities, personnel, equipment, scheduling, and community relations. Administrator develops curriculum, director participates in fund raising. *Preparation:* College degree with credits in administration. Experience in education and athletics helpful. *Compensation:* $10,000–$30,000+. *Job Outlook:* Good.

Reprinted by permission of the American Alliance for Health, Physical Education, Recreation and Dance, 1900 Association Drive, Reston, VA 22091.

Sources

AIAW Directory (athletic scholarships—1980–81). Association for Intercollegiate Athletics for Women, 1201 16th Street, N.W., Washington, DC 20036.

Careers in Physical Education and Sport (#245–06082), prepared by NASPE, NAGWS of AAHPERD. AAHPERD Publications, Dept. C, P.O. Box 704, 44 Industrial Park Circle, Waldorf, MD 20601.

Fahey, Thomas D., *What to Do About Athletic Injuries,* ed. by C. Castellano. Butterick Publishing, 1979.

Fixx, James F., *The Complete Book of Running.* Random House, 1977.

Good Housekeeping Woman's Almanac, ed. by Barbara McDowell and Hana Umlauf. Newspaper Enterprise Association, 1977.

Michener, James A., *Sports in America.* Random House, 1976.

Parkhouse, Bonnie L., and Lapin, Jackie, *Women Who Win: Exercising Your Rights in Sports.* Prentice-Hall, 1980.

"Recreation Specialist and Related Jobs." U.S. Civil Service Commission, Washington DC 20415, Announcement No. AC-5–04, 1976.

Runner's World. World Publications, Box 366, Mountain View, CA 94040.

Ullyot, Dr. Joan, *Women's Running.* Anderson World, 1976.

USTA College Tennis Guide. USTA Education and Research Center, 729 Alexander Road, Princeton, NJ 08540.

Women's Sports Annual Scholarship Guide. 314 Town and Country Village, Palo Alto, CA 94301.

Index

About the Author

GAIL ANDERSEN MYERS is a free-lance writer whose work appears in magazines and newspapers. She is an enthusiastic spectator of sports as well as a participant who enjoys skiing, golfing, sailing, swimming, and tennis. Other interests are travel, reading, and needlework.

Mrs. Myers has coached softball, managed a girls' tennis team, been a Girl Scout and 4-H leader and an elementary school teacher.

She is the wife of a weekend athlete and is the mother of two athletic daughters. The family lives in Huntingdon Valley, Pennsylvania.